ANSWERS

The Way It Has Always Been

J.P. MOORE

LAHREN JAMES PUBLISHING

LAHREN JAMES PUBLISHING
P.O. Box 2273
Station B
London, Ontario
N6A 4E3

National Library of Canada Cataloguing in Publication Data

Moore, J.P. (James Patrick), 1965-
Answers: the way it has always been

ISBN 0-9688950-0-X

1. Wisdom. 2. Conduct of life. 3. Self-help technique. I. Title

BJ1581.2.M66 2001 158.1 C2001-901619-0

Printed in Canada

Dedication

I wrote this for you.

ACKNOWLEDGEMENTS

I would like to thank God first and foremost for giving us the answers. I hope that I have done them justice. I would like to thank my wife for her patience and encouragement. To Chad Krulicki and Graham Duncan, thank you for your creativity and your input. It would not have been the same book without you.

PREFACE

As the dedication stated, I wrote this for you. I wrote this for everybody. I have had the world in my mind for ten years. Every struggle it has encountered, every pain it has felt and every mistake it has made has kept me writing because I knew that just about everything people were experiencing was preventable if only they knew the things that are written here. I also knew that this information all but guaranteed those things the world holds so precious. Great health, prosperity, peace and successful relationships are all simply a matter of course.

If you read this as you would any other book, you will be disappointed. The paragraphs will fly by, the chapters will end and you will have missed the meaning. Nothing presented here is either obvious or mastered, and it will take a great deal of effort on your part to see what others are not even looking for. Wisdom is not attained in a day.

This book has been my life and passion for more than a decade. I am, however, a reluctant writer; I have still not overcome my feelings of inadequacy to writing about such a subject. After all, I do not consider myself to be a wise man. I only wish that I were. This book is entirely based on the wisdom found in the Bible and, in particular, the book of Proverbs. While you read, you will find that there are times when I have used complete excerpts, concepts and imagery to demonstrate a point without citing the Bible explicitly. To do so would have destroyed the ebb and flow of the work and resulted in a completley different outcome.

Please let this acknowledgement stand for citation purposes. I have also decided to use the masculine gender in many cases for the simplicity and clarity. Please excuse these literary licenses.

About The Author

Who am I to tell you these things? I am nobody. I shall pass on just like all those before me, and history shall not remember my name. If you wish, let your imagination conjure an image of anyone you would like, and let him read to you the things that are written here.

PART I

Where Freedom Begins

Introduction

The sunrise always peels back the darkness of night.

If I were God, I would drive over to my friend's house tonight and cure her of her cancer. I would show up at her doorstep with her favorite flowers (she loves flowers) and when she answered, I would give her a big hug, kiss her on the forehead, and make it go away. If I were God, I would make it all go away — all of it. I would stop all wars, end all hunger, eliminate all disease and fill the world with love and peace the likes of which have not been seen since the beginning. I would recreate Eden.

The new Garden would be filled with the scents of spring and the sight of wildflowers in the fields nearby. Its beautiful mountain vistas would steal your breath away; the tranquility of slowly meandering rivers would soothe the souls of some while the raging pulse of white water would entice the tastes of others. Peering from cliffs of ancient cedar forests, you would see the endless patience of white, glacial fingers marching across landscapes of time.

The smell of hot apple pie and chocolate chip cookies would waft in lazy afternoon breezes and the succulent tastes of gourmet meals would delight you — as a bonus, you could eat all you want.

Golden sunsets on turquoise oceans would precede the violet beginnings of tropical evenings and white sand beaches would wrap you in a blanket of complete content-

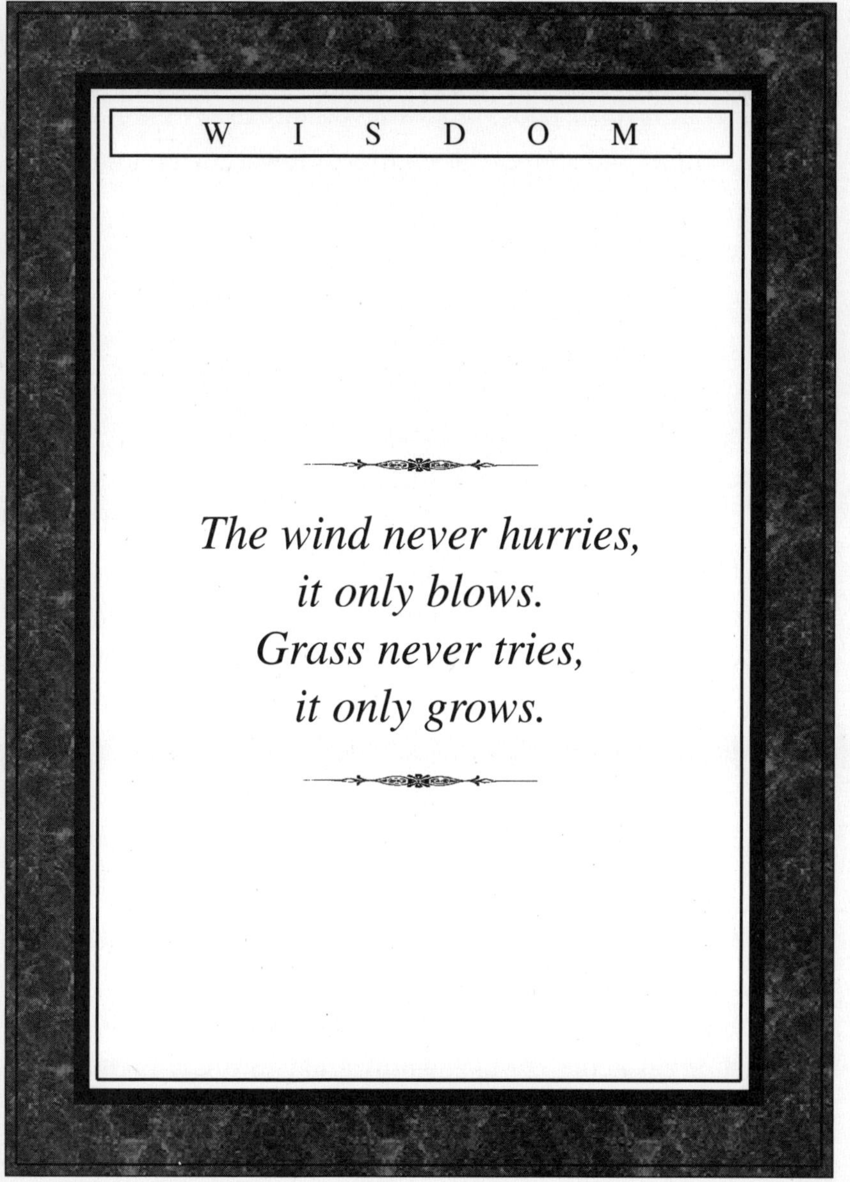

W I S D O M

The wind never hurries,
it only blows.
Grass never tries,
it only grows.

ment. You would hold hands as you walked barefoot with your love and every kiss would hold the same passion as the first kiss of a timeless romance.

At night, your pet would fall asleep on your lap as you read your favorite book, in your favorite chair, by the crackling sounds and soft, mellow glow of a warm and inviting fireplace.

An orchestra of birds would announce the day and a symphony of crickets would summon the night.

On Wednesday, you could picnic and watch the wind play across golden fields of barley. On Thursday you could observe elephants on the Serengeti and on Friday contemplate the silence of snow falling in the Andes.

No one would ever get sick; no one would ever die. I would protect you and I would love you, your friends and your family. I would even come to visit from time to time; we would sit around a campfire watching the fireflies late at night and I would answer all of your questions. Everyone would win the lottery.

But, clearly I am not God. I am not even close. And unfortunately, my ability to eliminate pain and suffering in this world is limited to the smiles that I give, the way that I treat people and the words that I have written in these pages.

It humbles me at how small my strength is and, on nights like these, tests my ability as a man to control my emotions as I consider the painful struggles of my friend. It is on days like these that I am reminded of the reason I have written this book: if I can help you avoid the trials of life, I may be able to give you a little piece of Eden.

* * * *

When I was young man, I stumbled across a collection of the most powerful truths ever written and it changed my life completely. I will never forget that night. I remember the intoxication of the words that I read and the powerful feelings of truth, hope, strength and certainty that overwhelmed me. The years that followed were filled with study and practice and great change. Every day was better than the day before because suddenly I had answers to the questions that had frustrated me my whole life. I suddenly knew why things were the way they were and are the way they are.

Ten years ago, I noticed patterns in the collection and began the long and arduous task of trying to organize and distill the information they contained into an enlightening and entertaining work. This book is the result.

In a way, it is a book that will give you complete insight into the difficulties we face during our lifetime. If you are like me, you will shake your head as you read it and wish you could have known what is written here much earlier on in life. It would have made things much, much easier.

Life is a mystery. For a lucky few, it is ecstasy. For most, it is routine. For others it is tragedy. Frequently, it masquerades as the words *promise* and *hope* while pushing us to the limits of our resolve and our ability to cope. For common men such as myself, life can be a struggle; we yearn but rarely achieve.

Looking at history, we find that life is an endless tale

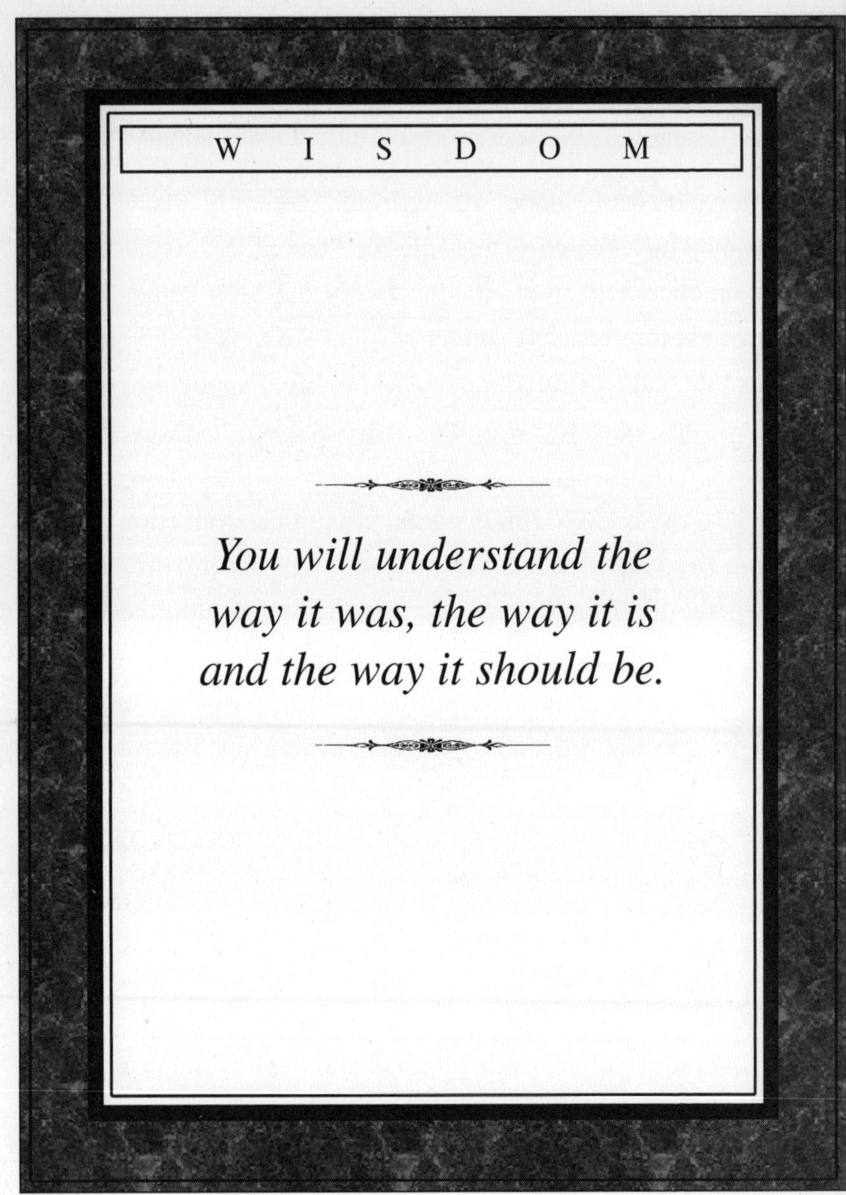
W I S D O M
You will understand the way it was, the way it is and the way it should be.

of old stories retold again and again. The problems you and I face are the same, more or less, as those faced by people living thousands of years ago. Though the faces and the times change, the paths people choose are worn and weary from the billions of anxious and troubled feet that have trod their way. The question is why do we choose the paths we choose?

As a simple man, I know only too well that it is possible to be wise in some areas and foolish in most. I have been where you are and I know your pain. But if you will trust me just a little, I will take you from where you are today to where you want to be. I will show you why you are where you are and lead you down much better paths. I will introduce you to wisdom.

I am not a pious man, and despite this book's being a synthesis of the wisdom found in the book of Proverbs, I never intended it to be spiritual by design. Its purpose is to be extremely practical in order to ease a world of pain and avoid a lot of needless suffering. It is the only way that my life and what I know can be used to help you.

Smiling at you doesn't help you get out of debt. Being polite to you doesn't help your marriage. Only wisdom can help you solve these problems. Only wisdom can change your life. History has proven this so.

Wisdom is as it always has been. It is clarity, harmony and peace. Each word embraces your heart and your mind so completely that it is as if a sudden and irrevocable surge of awareness threatens to overwhelm you. Life itself seems to spring from its hauntingly, beautiful words, and

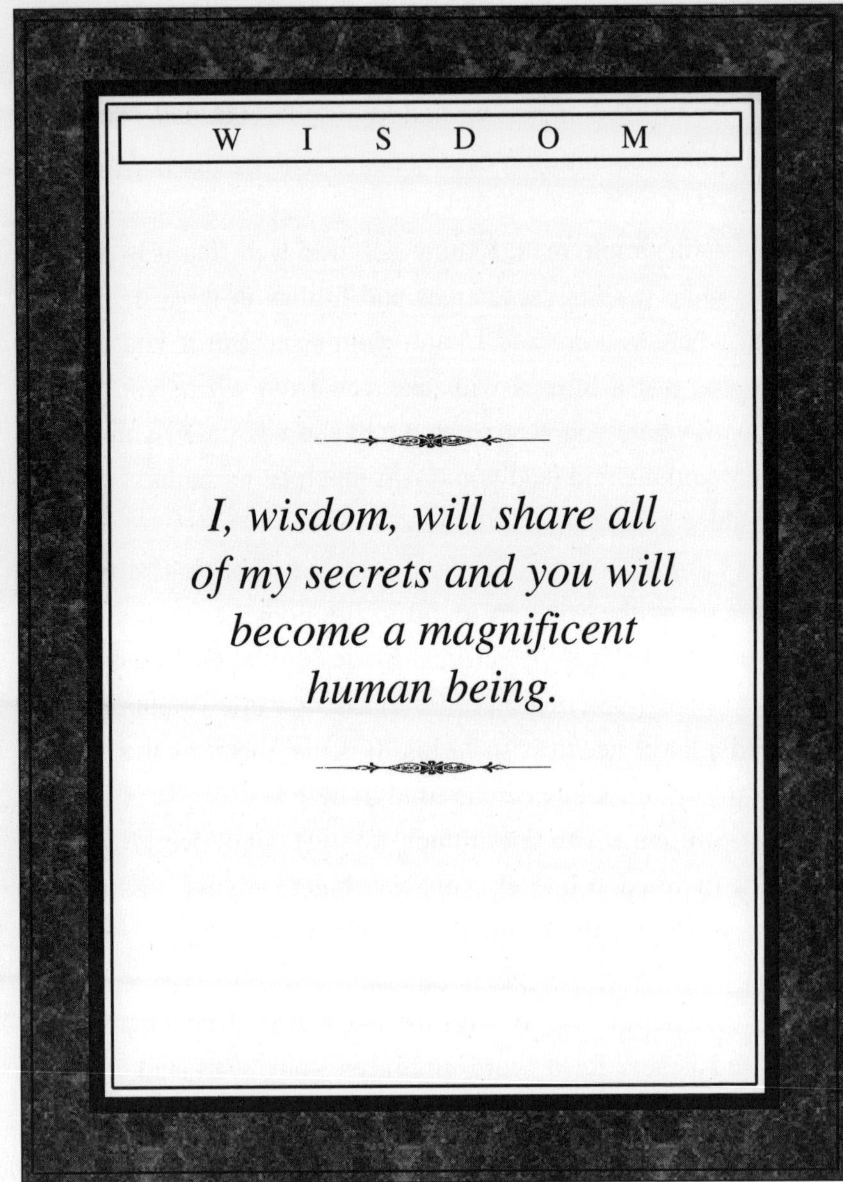
W I S D O M
I, wisdom, will share all of my secrets and you will become a magnificent human being.

the understanding that accompanies it is unlike anything you will ever experience. Every insight provides another application; every observation builds towards enlightenment.

With wisdom comes lucidity of thought and correct intent. As wisdom takes hold, so too do its ways. Justice lives in you. Faith becomes an emotion - not a word. You dole out truth, love and kindness as if it were candy to children and go to bed at night with the comfort of knowing you did everything right by man and by God and your sleep becomes carefree.

I have found that every single person on this planet has a reason for being here. I've known for many years that this book is the reason I am here. With a wry smile, I look back upon events that the universe has conjured in order that I complete these pages. Since that night when I came across my first glance at wisdom, I have been burned in some of life's extraordinary fires to bring you this book. It is the price I had to pay in order to truly know what it was I was writing about. All I can say is that anything of significance in life is in these pages. I hope you find what you are looking for.

CONSEQUENCES

There are few great lives. A great life is for the great at heart.

We will never grasp the complexity of this universe—the weave and tapestry of lives and history, past and future in perfect blend. Thus, we can never judge the way of things, for fate and choice mingle with time and space on this planet in ways unforeseen and unimaginable.

This is a world of consequences. Each day's decisions ripple across the oceans of our lives to reveal to us the sublime nature of the human experience. From the moment of our birth it has been all up to us and yet it has been entirely out of our hands. Since the dawn of man it has been this way.

If you sit atop the hourglass of time and gaze upon the history of our struggles, you will find before you thousands of years of pain and suffering of global proportion. You will see war and you will see strife. You will see disaster and disease. In the cities below, you will find the same; political wars and political strife, social disaster and social disease. In the houses in the city, you will see people at war and marriage strife, personal disasters and personal disease. In the mirror of your bathroom, you will find a lifetime of pain; internal wars and the memories of strife, your own disasters and your own disease.

The history of struggle, it seems, is the reiteration of similar lives; old stories that suffer the same painful end-

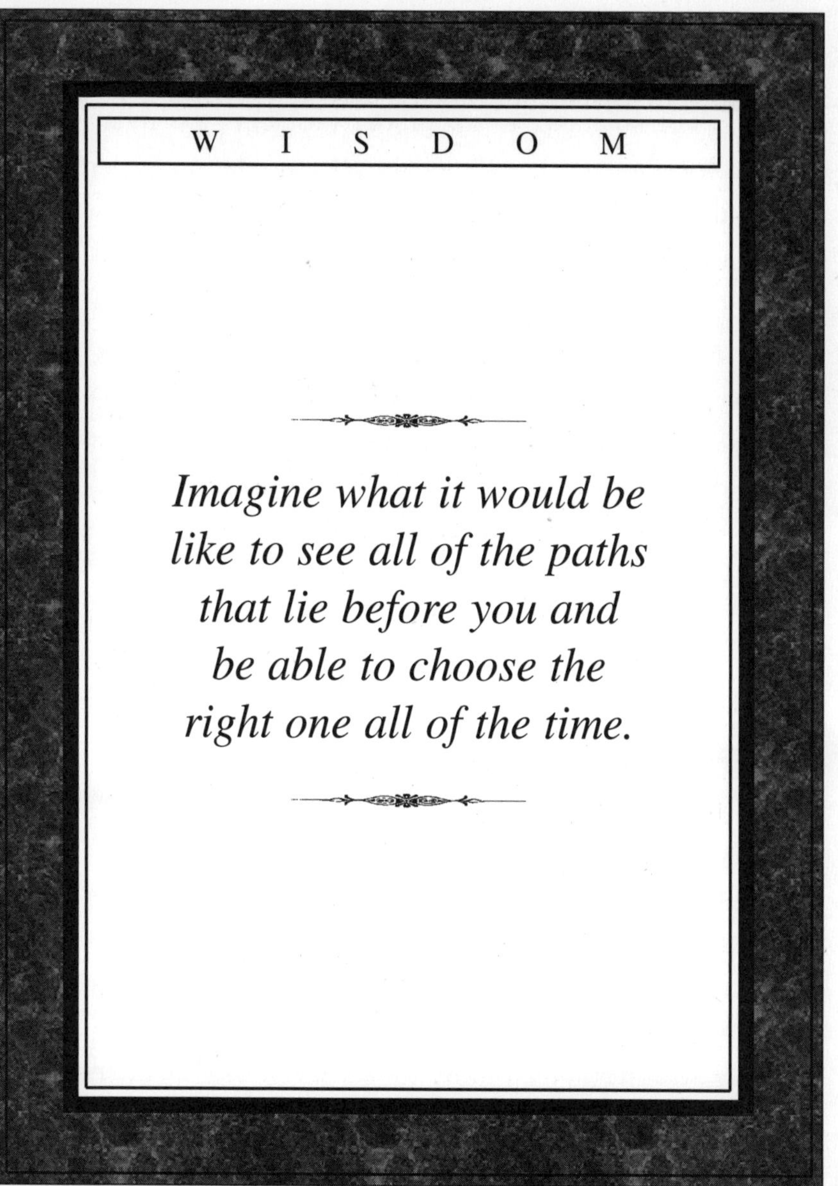

W I S D O M

Imagine what it would be like to see all of the paths that lie before you and be able to choose the right one all of the time.

ings. The tales are written with different characters but the plot is always the same. The mistakes our parents made, we make, and the mistakes our parents made were made thousands of years ago.

The solutions to all of our problems are relatively simple to solve for individuals yet considering the entire population as a whole, the solutions are six billion strong in complexity.

It is here that we find the challenge. Individually, we are responsible for the human condition and are charged with living exemplary lives. We cannot, however, force a planet filled with people to do the right thing at all times.

We look but we do not see; we listen but we do not hear; we live but we do not understand.

Almost all of us walk steadfast in our own convictions, intellectually and emotionally blind to consequences, yet fail to see the wake of chaos behind us that foreshadows the regret to come. With great and foolish bias, we walk along paths that seem right to us, ever confident in our own uneducated and irrational ways even when the errors are painfully obvious for all to see.

I've lived this. I think we all have lived this. I cringe at how blind I was in my youth. If only I could have seen more clearly. If only I had been more insightful and been able to see past my childish arrogance to notice the diffi-

W I S D O M

Imagine what it would be like to be the calm in the center of the storm.

culties that people around me were having. I could have eased their burdens instead of adding to them. Sadly, my behavior was deplorable at times and my opinions both uneducated and impetuous. I wish I could have been a better man. The memories would be so much sweeter.

We are all this way. We live by blaming others and hide behind a bound and gagged conscience. We look but we do not see; we listen but we do not hear; we live but we do not understand.

Thus, the few that are wise are suffocated by the troubled lives of the masses. The peaceful ripples they produce are reflected back upon them in torrents of mockery and injustice as the history of suffering continues to repeat itself.

Much in this world is born of personal pain. It does not have to be this way but it is the way it has always been. We create the problems; we affect the lives of others, allowing our own faults to spill over into society, and suffer the consequences that inevitably come from our actions. It is here that we find that most of life's problems are a consequence, not a punishment, though they often feel the same. We set our self up and this world furnishes the fall, every time.

A woman I know is learning this right now. She is a loving wife and a proud mother of two. She has been a smoker all of her life, however, lives on junk food and never exercises. Several years ago, she moved from a low-pressure work environment into a position that is both challenging and extremely stressful. Predictably, her health broke

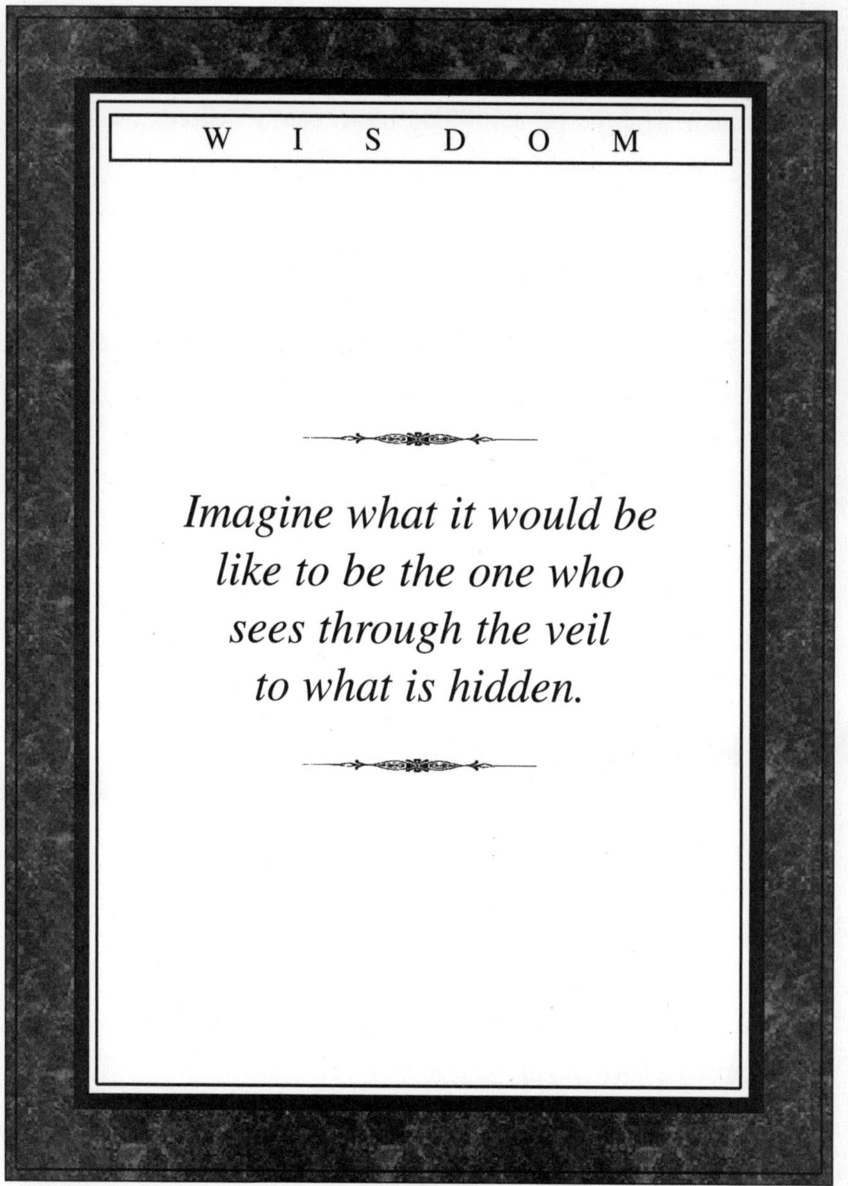
WISDOM
Imagine what it would be
like to be the one who
sees through the veil
to what is hidden.

under the strain and she spent six weeks in bed trying to recover from the choices she had made. Her husband and children struggled every day with the worry that a sick wife and mother create; and the company she works for strained to cover the extra workload that she imposed on her coworkers.

Ultimately, her body, her family, her company or all three will compel her to change under the guise of pain and force her down a better path. Pain will break her just as pain has broken billions of people before her. No one is immune.

...my troubles were the offspring of a life poorly lived.

But it doesn't have to be this way. She could just as easily eat a well balanced diet, quit smoking, exercise and find a job that challenges her without undue stress. She knows this; she is a very bright woman. It is just that she is not very wise. She can't see.

Almost all of us find God in times of our greatest pain. Everyone finds God eventually. The consequences of our actions are simply too great and the pain too unbearable to avoid what lies beyond an uneasy conscience.

The little inconveniences in life question our resolve, difficulties pry at our beliefs and dire circumstances reveal the conflict we have with The Almighty. Our own vanity,

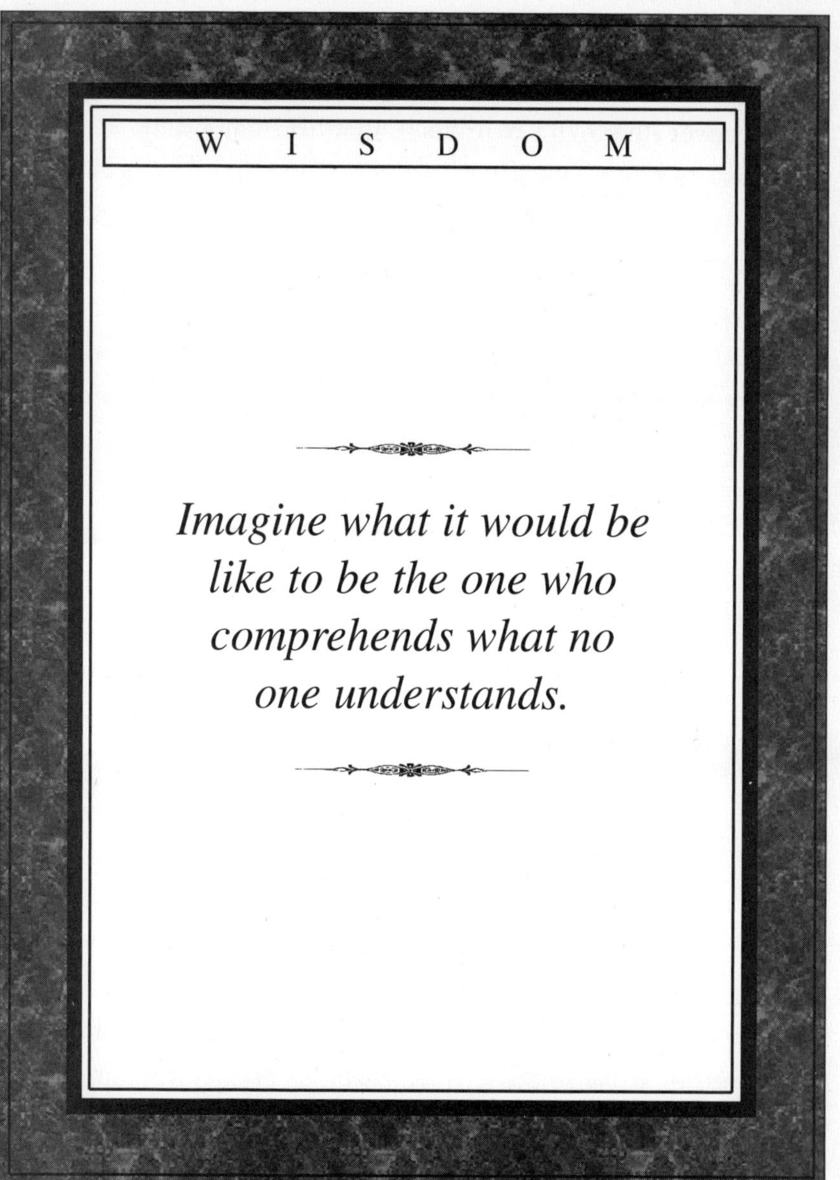

W I S D O M

Imagine what it would be like to be the one who comprehends what no one understands.

greed and foolishness create our troubles; and yet our heart rages against God as if He is the source of our problems. I remember.

It was winter. I could see that the many faces of wrong had paid a visit to my life and a part of me became aware that it was my fault. I was quite ill at the time and decided to see if the small voice of conscience that had been poking and prodding me was part of a bigger picture.

Knowing that my troubles were the offspring of a life poorly lived, I could not blame God. I realized that, at the very least, I should respect the God I did not know and the ways I did not understand. I should be astonished at the complexity of this universe and try to grasp the notion that there was, in fact, a divine genius behind the masterpiece, and all I was doing was making it difficult to paint. In this state of mind, I took my first step towards a much better life. In the silence of my room, tired and shivering, I said a quiet prayer and asked that the faces turn away.

* * * *

All things great or small have beginnings; nothing is inconsequential. The beginnings of all good things seem insignificant. Look to the poor man who saves a penny out of the first dime he earns. He saves a dime out of a dollar and a dollar out of the first ten dollars that pass through his hands. Inconsequential — one dollar and eleven cents. However, the habit carried on for years to come will transform the impoverished — guaranteed!

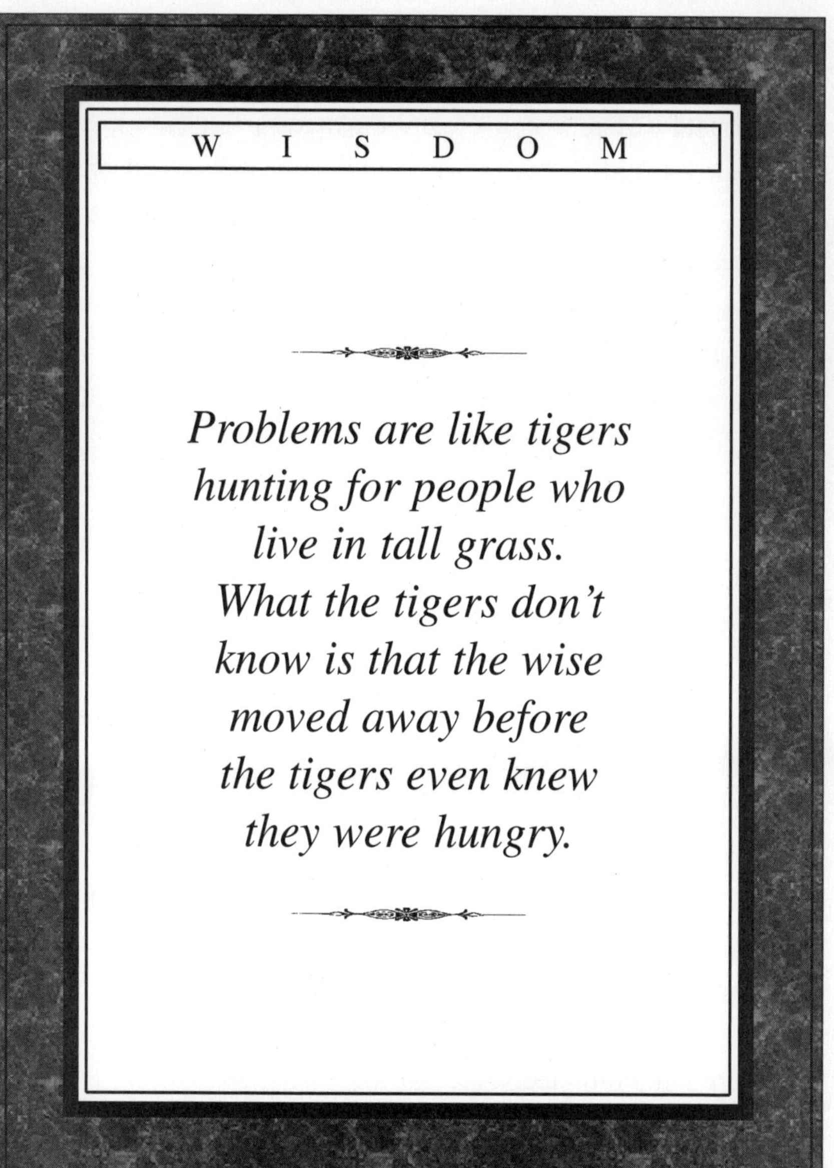
W I S D O M
Problems are like tigers
hunting for people who
live in tall grass.
What the tigers don't
know is that the wise
moved away before
the tigers even knew
they were hungry.

The beginnings of all downfalls seem trivial. Alcoholism begins with the first drink, poverty with the first frivolous choice and divorce with the first careless thought or deed.

By way of example, let me tell you a familiar story of subtle beginnings but all too predictable consequences.

You are sitting in a bar with your friends talking about the old times. You have been a trucker for sixteen years and aside from a speeding ticket you got from an overzealous cop in Alabama four years prior, your record is clean and you are well respected among your colleagues. You are, what some would call, a gamer. You never miss a delivery; you are professional and a real credit to truckers across North America.

From day one, you have made it a point to not drink while en route but on this one particular Friday night in August, you decide to bend this personal rule because one of your friends is having his fiftieth birthday. One drink becomes two and two becomes five. The party is great but it has been many years since you could boast about being an *accomplished drinker* and the night proves difficult to say the least. As a result, you wake up several hours behind schedule with a hangover that reminds you of the reasons why you don't drink much anymore.

By the time you hit the road it is a very hot, muggy afternoon. Fortunately, the traffic seems light and you figure you will press your luck a little to make up lost time. You still have two days to get to where you need to be, but it is going to be real tight from here on in.

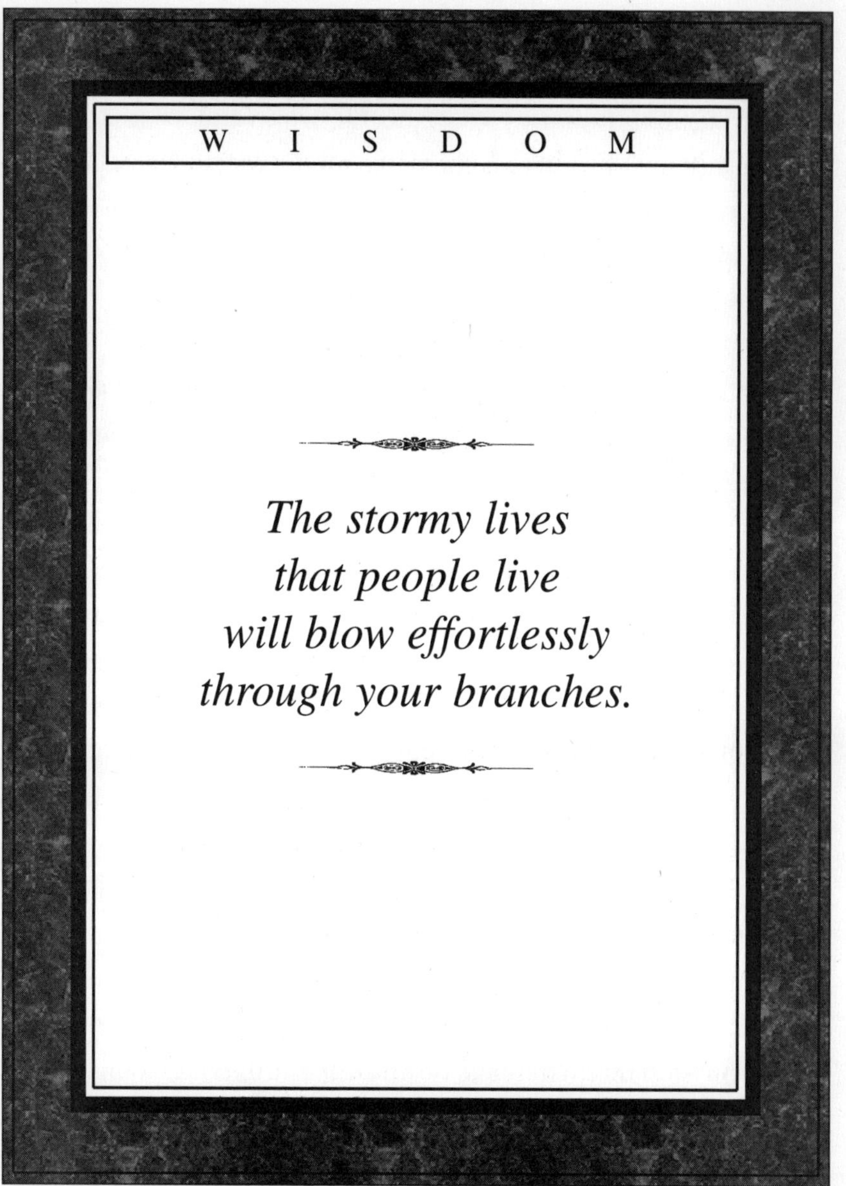

W I S D O M

The stormy lives
that people live
will blow effortlessly
through your branches.

On a typical, busy interstate highway, your life suddenly converges with the lives of many other people as you enter an off-ramp with too much speed, your load shifts and the rig rolls over onto the merging traffic. In your side mirror, the last thing you see, as the world and your stomach turn upside down, is the panic on the faces of an elderly couple (on their way to their grandson's eighth birthday) disappear beneath the back end of your truck as your entire load crushes their vehicle and kills the couple instantly.

The two cars that are driving directly behind the elderly couple careen wildly to avoid the accident and slam violently into the metal guardrail. Two more die; another is critically injured. The next six cars, tailgating as most do on the interstate, collide, sending two vehicles into the adjacent drainage ditch while the remaining four tangled cars completely block the southbound lane. Two people suffer whiplash, one severely injures his lower back; the remaining are simply lucky. Within an hour, traffic is backed up for twelve miles. There are no other exits.

The two that die are a couple in their late twenties. They leave behind three young children, a small life insurance policy and a large mortgage. The children spend the rest of their childhood in foster care. The critically injured gentleman is the head of the sales department of a small automation firm. In his satchel lies a government tender submission that will make or break the struggling company he works for. Due to the nature of the tender process, only hard-copy submissions are acceptable and there can be no extensions beyond the twelve-noon deadline. There are no

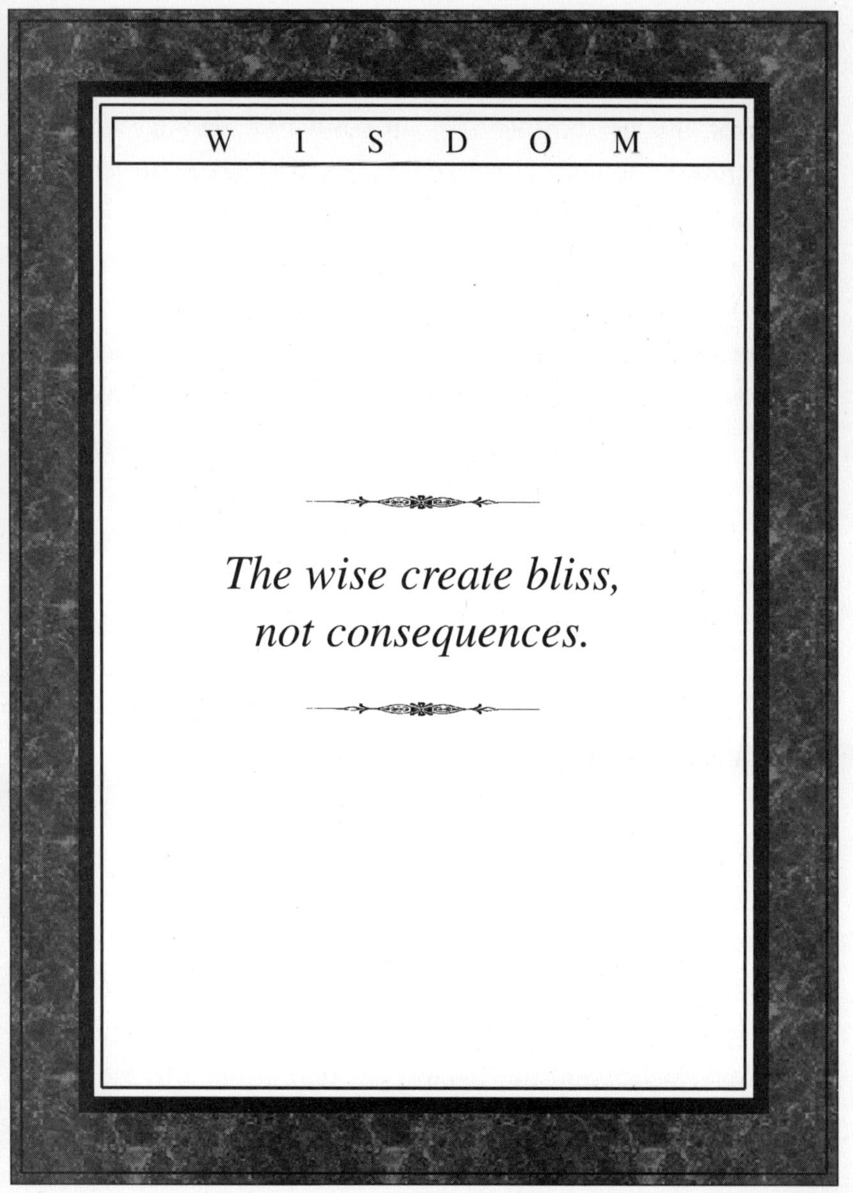
W I S D O M
The wise create bliss,
not consequences.

exceptions. Everything was riding on this bid.

He never makes the delivery, the project goes to another bidder and the small automation firm declares bankruptcy the following day. His head injuries are so severe that he remains in a coma for two weeks, suffers temporary blindness and undergoes three reconstructive surgeries to repair the damage from the accident.

Meanwhile, there is a fire in a local school. With most rescue vehicles committed to the accident scene, a fire crew must be dispatched from an adjacent town. Unfortunately, the crew arrives much later than the local crew would have, and a four-year old little girl perishes in the fire. The inquest that follows reveals that, if the accident hadn't occurred, the local fire crew would have arrived a full ten minutes earlier and would likely have saved her. The mother of the little girl, having lost a sister to fire when she was a teenager, goes into shock and is hospitalized in a psychiatric ward for the next three years. In the mean time, her job and her marriage disintegrate from the stress.

Over ten thousand cars are caught in the traffic jam; nearly fifteen thousand people are subject to hours of delays. Cars overheat, appointments are missed, tempers flare. Like ripples in a pond, the accident touches nearly one hundred thousand lives that day both directly and indirectly. The six o'clock news plays footage of the twisted wreckage and police and fire fighters are once again affected by gruesome images that would haunt them the rest of their lives.

Emergency crews pull you from the wreckage and

W I S D O M
Wisdom is twenty-twenty foresight.

place you on a stretcher for transport to the nearest hospital. In the accident, you suffer a concussion, dislocate a shoulder and break your left leg in three places.

The shoulder heals fine but the left knee develops arthritis several years later.

Your career as a truck driver ends that day. Your license is suspended and you are sued beyond your means to pay.

All first steps are indeed the largest.

The images of the elderly couple being crushed beneath your truck and the deaths of all of the others continually haunt you. Although alcohol created your problems, alcohol becomes your crutch and ultimate downfall.

For the next twelve years, you labor in a manufacturing plant making a living doing piece work. Your marriage does not survive. The money you had set aside to send your two daughters to college is spent in lawyer's fees and doctor bills. Both girls marry young and neither fulfills her dream of going to college. You die of liver disease at fifty-seven.

It never ceases to amaze me how such insignificant decisions can produce such tragic endings.

We will all suffer from the chaos of other people's decisions at one time or another. It is inevitable. There are a

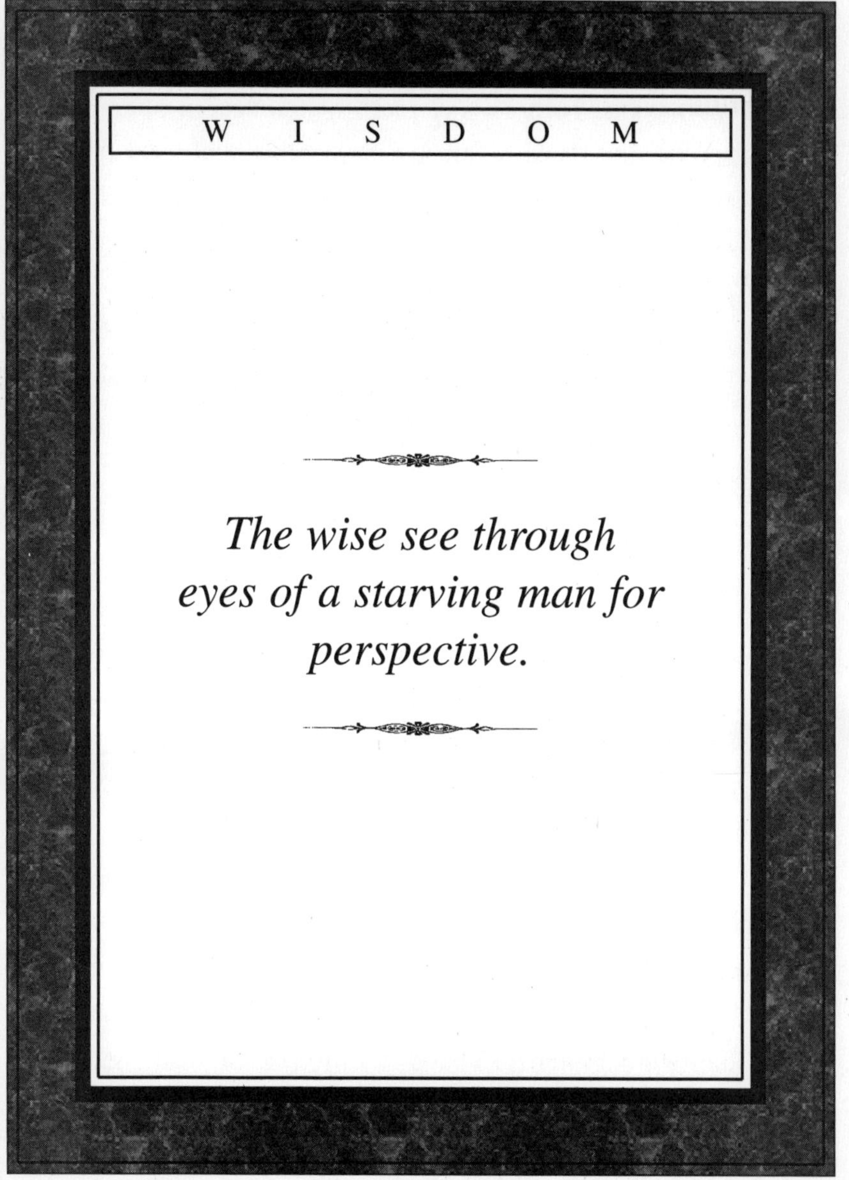
W I S D O M
The wise see through
eyes of a starving man for
perspective.

lot of people and there are a lot of plans, each with its own agenda, be it good, bad or indifferent.

We will encounter the chaos that is the result of individuality struggling to push towards goals that defy the common good. Turn on any radio or television, open any newspaper and there before us, mired in the struggle, lies this inevitability.

* * * *

We seek, we crave, we search and we desire. Invariably, we find what our choices lead us to. Those who seek, find. Those who do not seek, find anyway; and the path known as "anyway" is seldom an easy place to walk.

Great canyons start with a single drop of water; the mighty oak from the acorn.

I see this everyday. My office is located in the heart of the city. Homeless and successful people alike walk on the same sidewalks, breathe the same air and have the same opportunities. A lifetime of poor choices, however, results in one man begging for change. A lifetime of wise choices enables another man to live his dreams and avoid the pain and embarrassment that all of the other paths include as part of the journey.

W I S D O M
Inconvenience is understood,
not criticized.

On your journey, you have responsibilities. You have the responsibility to remain healthy so that you do not burden your family and society economically, physically or emotionally. You have the responsibility of self-education. You and you alone are responsible for truly knowing and truly understanding. It is not the responsibility of your teachers, your parents, your government or your friends. It is up to you.

Every step you take in your development is solitary. Though there may be many choices to consider, the decisions are yours alone. Without the persistent attention to all of the details in your life, weeds grow, fire burns and wind blows where it may. Without discipline, it all falls apart.

Those who seek, find.
Those who do not seek, find anyway.

Daily consequences lead us to an inevitable end; but you have the freedom to choose wisely and choose what that inevitability shall be. Lazy hands make a man poor in time, poor in spirit, poor in health and poor in riches. Diligent hands, however, bring wealth in all aspects of life. Invest a little everyday and it will grow to the end you desire.

The examples are endless. Those who have made the wise commitment to stay healthy do what is necessary.

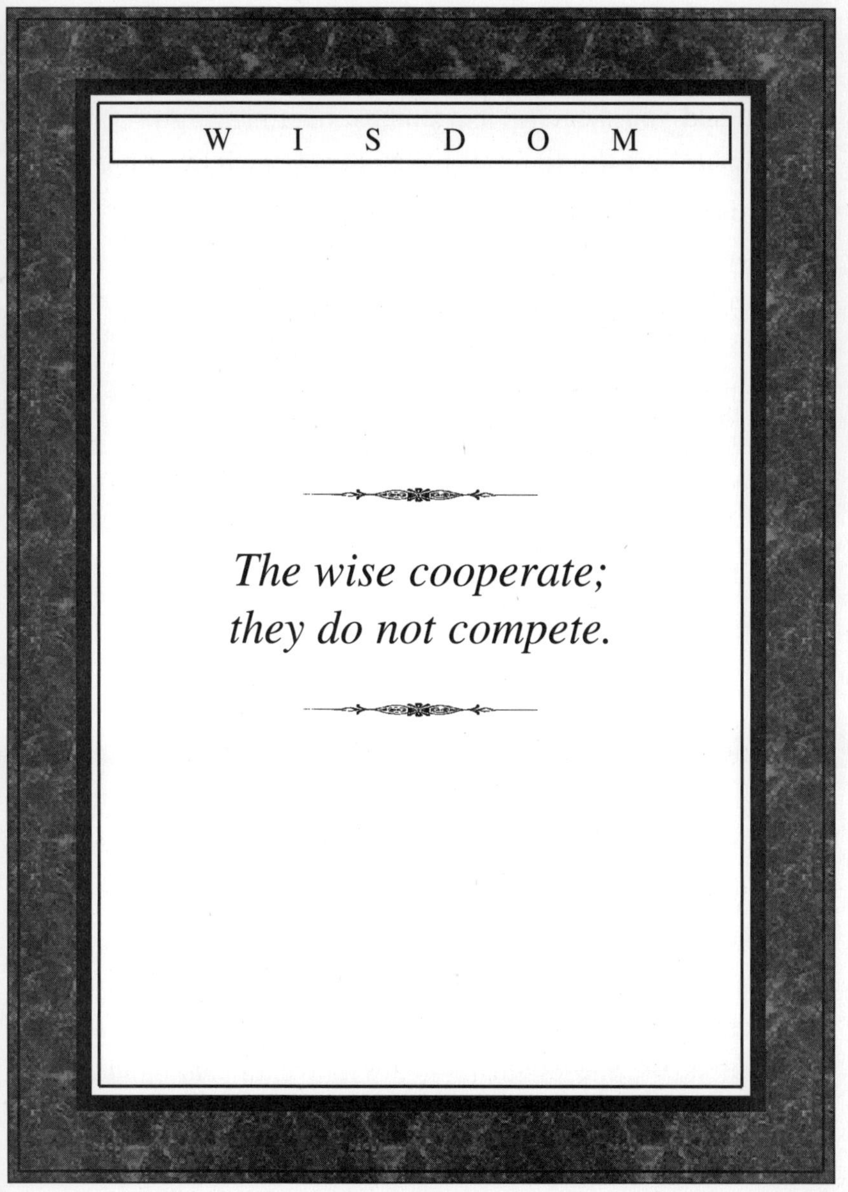
W I S D O M
The wise cooperate;
they do not compete.

They work at it and they reap the benefits of what they do. Those who are wise with the money they earn always have plenty. Those who value time spent with their family have a wonderful family to show for it.

Whether you trip and stumble or stride magnificently through your life is up to you. But know this. Discipline in the midst of chaos is easy while you are strong and the sun is shining. It is easy to smile when it is all going your way. Strength, however, is built in times of turmoil. In times of strife you must be the strength of the world, you must live on thoughts of a better life and a better way — you must be the light in the darkness.

Love the days when it all goes bad. Love the challenge and the struggle to improve. Cherish the times when your efforts don't seem to make any headway for it is in times like these that true progress is made. It is in times like these that wisdom is revealed.

If you have but little strength, then cultivate what you have and build upon it daily so that slowly, like a small stream on a granite landscape, given time and the faith known as patience, you will carve out the greatest of canyons in the hardest of rocks and all will marvel at your works.

The longings that are fulfilled as a result of your sustained efforts are like a tree of life and with them come new possibilities. Successful days burn forever in your mind coloring the way in which you think and approach the days to come. Doors open and ideas loom on the horizon. What was once difficult becomes simple; what was once impossible

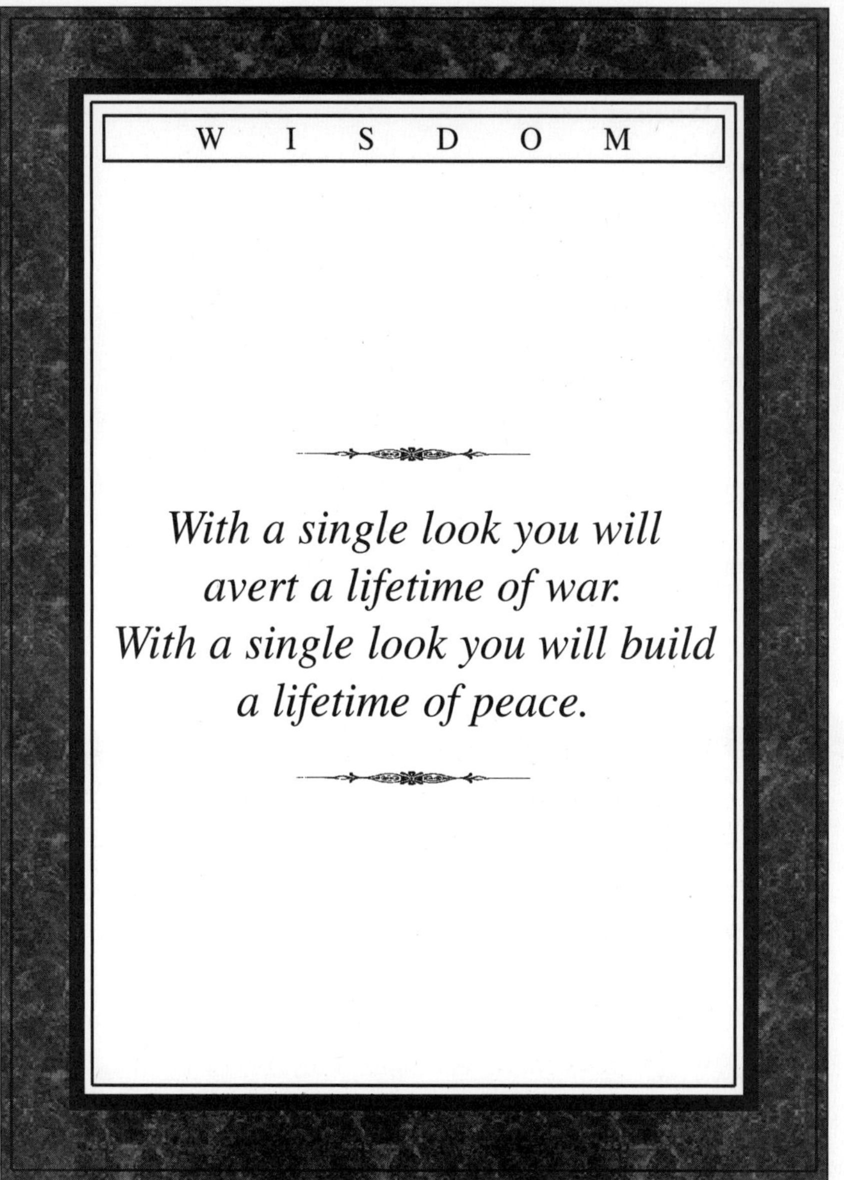

W I S D O M

With a single look you will
avert a lifetime of war.
With a single look you will build
a lifetime of peace.

will only require effort. With each fulfillment come further desires; they will stretch you and drive you and entice you to live.

W I S D O M
You will become a
consequential savant.

Subtle Slavery

The Earth cries for wasted days and wasted lives.

We are all subtle slaves of this world and until you can see the puppet masters pulling your strings, you will never be free.

To illustrate, consider our health. In a child's formative years, many succumb to peer pressure, develop bad habits and make choices that lay the foundation for poor health to come. Foolish youth, sly advertising, junk food, drugs, cigarettes and alcohol are a perfect combination for unscrupulous people with a taste for young money.

Over time our children become slaves to people and products that clearly do not have their best interests in mind. Instead of building their health on a foundation of rock, they build it on sand. Instead of strengthening their young bodies, they tear them down.

To young adults, more strings are added. Companies feed on the naive and desperate, talent and overtime are sacrificed to an uncaring employer for a pittance, and meaningless work stifles their spirit in exchange for a minimum wage.

Marketing masters create an artificial drive that panders to the emotional and physical desires of a juvenile populace and debt begins to accumulate. Overindulgence becomes the norm, sin slides in the back door, vanity replaces reason, ego begets pride, laziness strains against

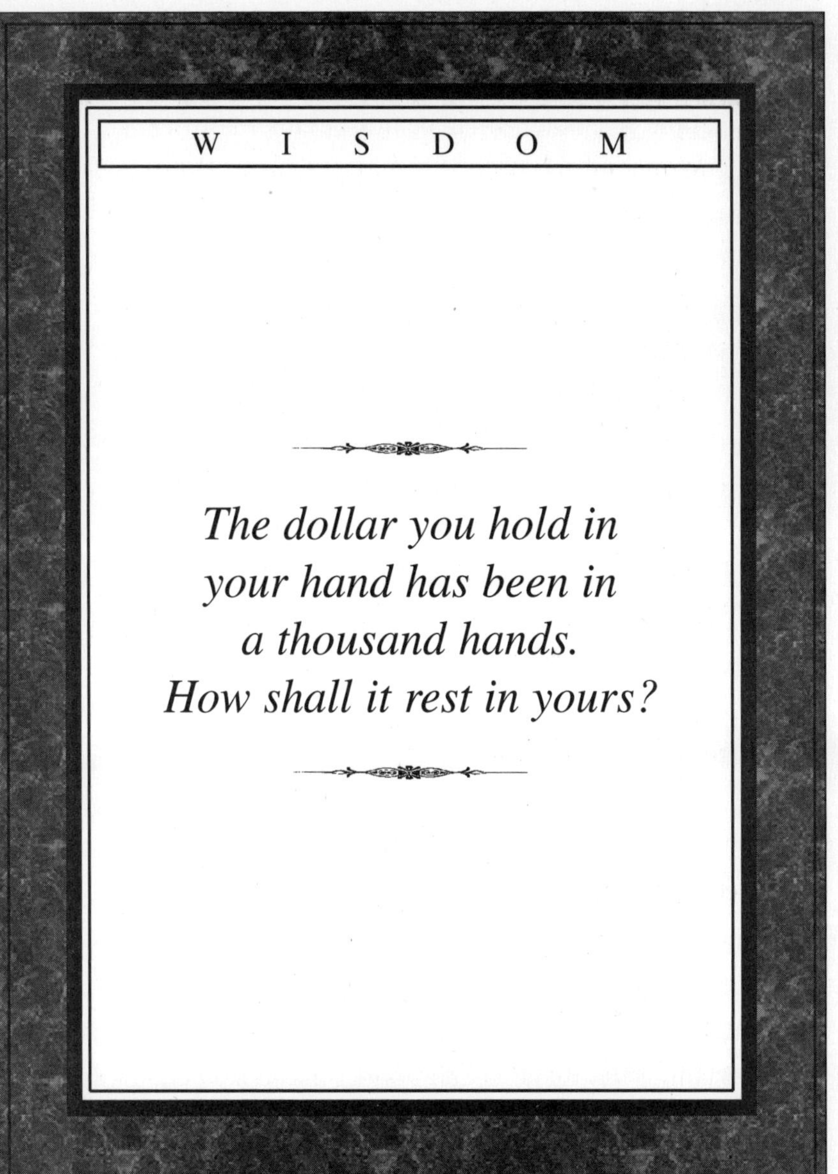
W I S D O M
The dollar you hold in
your hand has been in
a thousand hands.
How shall it rest in yours?

anxiousness and moderation becomes lost in a sea of beleaguered virtues.

History then takes its cue as the unforeseen consequences of ancient strings are added to the fray. Time passes, people get older, their health begins to suffer and life becomes a tangled web of knots. But fear not, for more web masters await. Living off of other people's pain, every snake oil salesman with a promising potion pulls another string and the predictable cycle of needless suffering goes to enrich another.

This, my friend, is subtle slavery, but instead of forced labor it is our unassuming ways that pay the world a little at a time to steal away our health, our wealth and our dignity.

Every string has two masters. Every string pulls in a different direction. Your wisdom (or lack thereof) is on one side, an opportunist is on the other, and your life is caught in between.

Every string has a price economically, socially, physically or spiritually. Laziness itself is a string that results in poor performance, missed opportunity, economic regret and tedious labor doing that which we do not want to do. Lack of skill and attention regarding financial affairs is another string that creates the impoverished and produces slaves to welfare, to poor jobs and dissatisfaction in life. Apathy towards relationships results in lost friends and family. Everything has its price and puppet masters await.

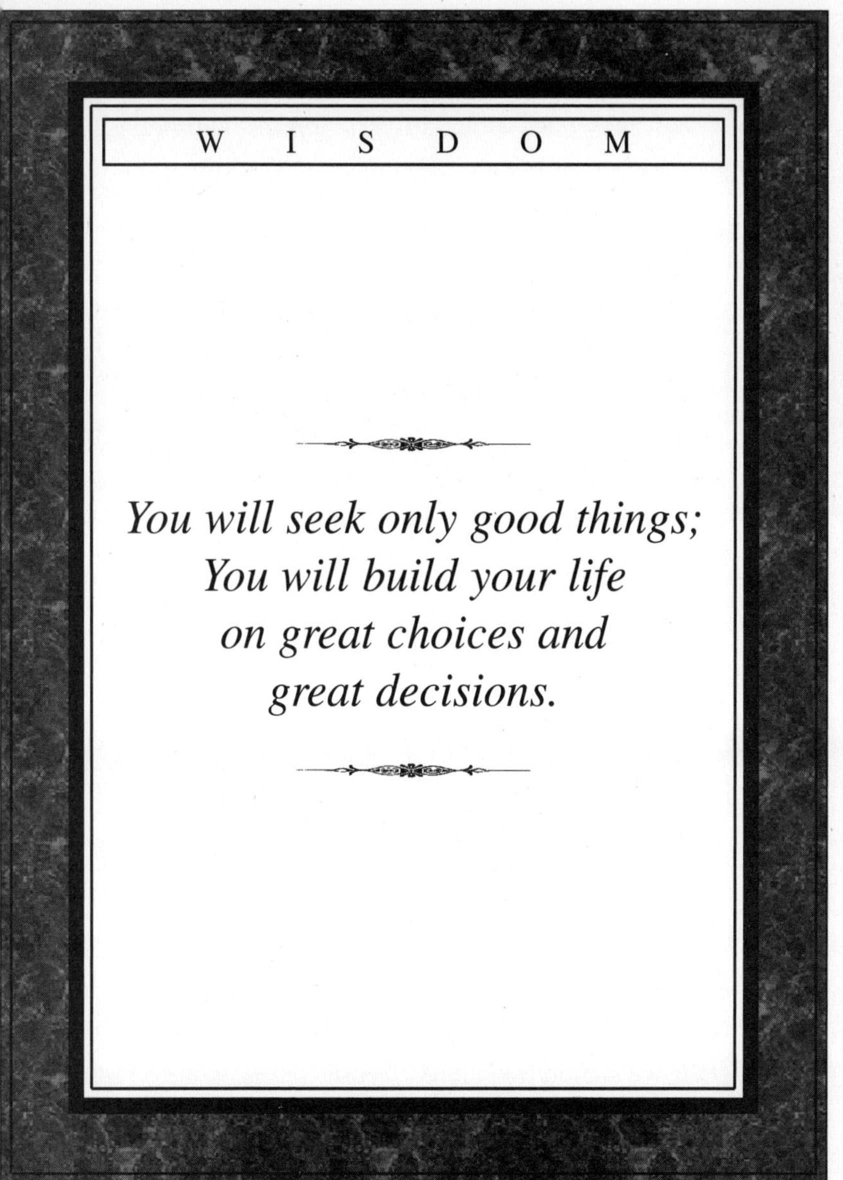

WISDOM

You will seek only good things;
You will build your life
on great choices and
great decisions.

For years, it seemed as if my jobs were a documentary of how work is not supposed to be. During my career, I have felt the sting of unjust employers and witnessed the rage and foolishness of corporate tyrants first hand. I have been mistreated, taken advantage of, overworked and underpaid. Rarely have I ever been treated as a valued human being.

You are worth so much more!

Having lived these experiences I now know what business is like and what it does to people. But, I also have some unique perspectives on what the workplace is supposed to be like.

If I were your boss, I would tell you that your life is valuable and mean it. I would appreciate your time, effort, skill and energy and your paycheck would reflect it. If you worked with me, I would promise to provide you with an environment that would allow you to grow and nurture your abilities. I would give you all the resources and training you require to do the best job that you can. I would empower you to become anything you want to become and together we would strive to build a company of great people. Together we would take care of your family, our community and contribute to the world we live in.

Few of us work in an environment like this. In fact, most shoulder the burden of meaningless work because,

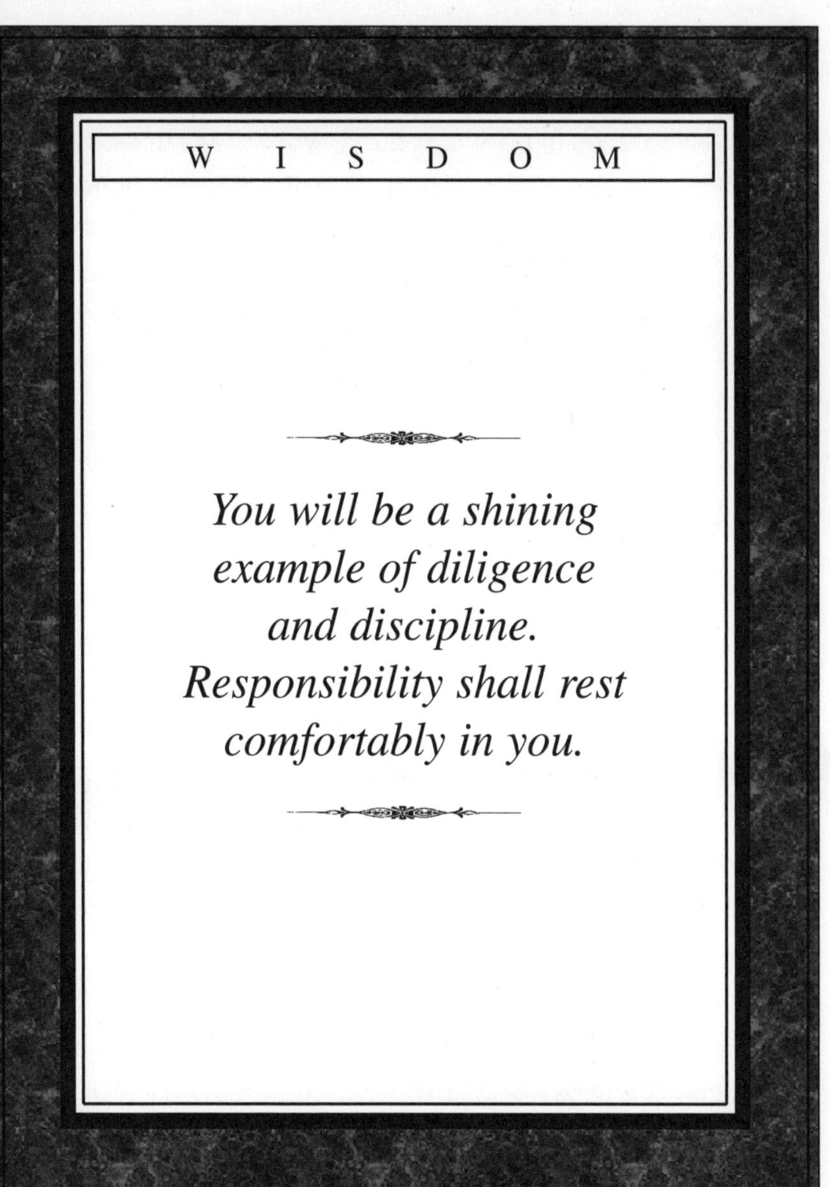

W I S D O M

You will be a shining example of diligence and discipline. Responsibility shall rest comfortably in you.

unfortunately, it is the only work that we have proven ourselves worthy to do.

I know what this is like. Most of my career was spent working hard on jobs that had no future. I've cleaned toilets, cut grass, dug graves, washed dishes, cooked, toiled in factories, been a draftsman, worked in sales, held government jobs and the list goes on. Regardless of the position, I put in long, hard days because it was in my nature to do so. It was only after I made a decisive and concentrated effort to improve my skills and my abilities, however, that everything changed.

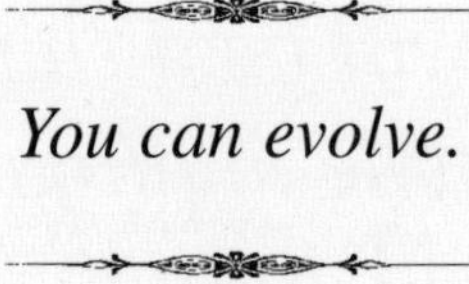

On the whole, few study to improve themselves. Few take the classes and seek out the knowledge to improve their lot in life. Even fewer sit down and design the life they want for themselves. Regrettably, there are great consequences to this.

Most of us end up sacrificing our lives, our time and our energies to make another person wealthy. We lend ourselves out to the nearest bidder. Not the highest bidder, not the bidder with the most character who could cultivate our talents and give us an environment that would allow us to grow — just the nearest bidder who would pay us and, at times, abuse us. To most, our work has been their luxury, to

W I S D O M

You will be nobody's slave;
you shall be free!

others, their waste.

A friend of mine reminded me of this. Where he worked, the leadership in the organization had turned a blind eye to corruption, incompetence and contemptible behavior, all working in disturbing collusion to maintain the status quo and quash the success of others. Though he tried in vain to be an exemplary employee, those in power above him and those who worked below made a mockery of his ideals and his values nearly everyday.

Slowly, he began to see the people for who they truly were and realized that the company was only using him. He knew that he deserved better and decided to move on to better people and better opportunities.

Why, he asked, do people in authority think they have the right to mistreat those who work under them? Why is it that, despite being just as flawed in their perceptions and abilities as the next man, people in authority always think they are right?

I recall a situation where I confronted a high-ranking executive about an employee. It had been repeatedly demonstrated that the employee was criminally negligent in his duties, incompetent, insubordinate, and a compulsive liar who mistreated those under him with great regularity. Yet, the executive promoted him!

People were livid over the move. His most trusted advisors could not believe the ridiculous decision that had been made.

When an inquiry was made into the promotion, his pride would not let him admit to making such a colossal

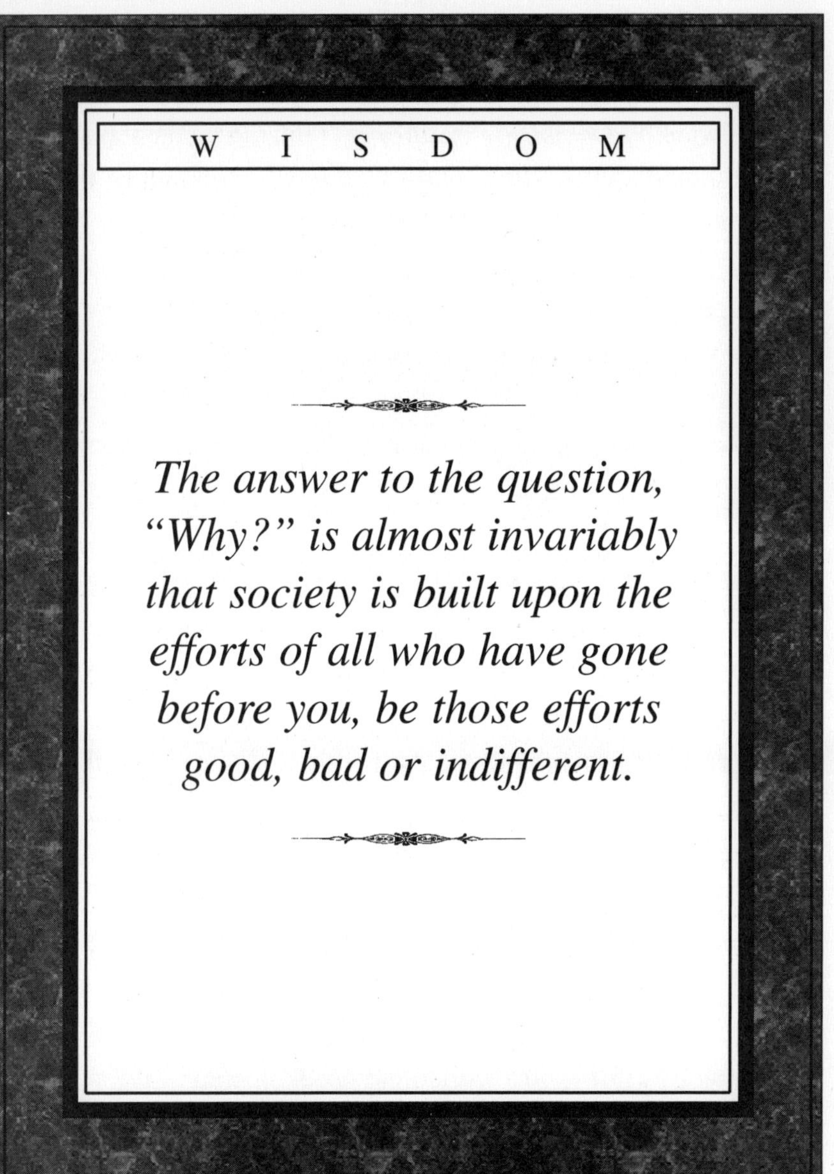

WISDOM

The answer to the question, "Why?" is almost invariably that society is built upon the efforts of all who have gone before you, be those efforts good, bad or indifferent.

mistake. You could see it in his eyes. He did everything he could to present the few redeeming qualities of the man he had promoted, and yet the justification was absolutely absurd given the weight of evidence against the employee. In fact, the executive had been given report after report detailing the problems with the employee, yet he tore a strip off any person questioning his authority.

Tragically, by defending the indefensible, he lost all of the credibility he had built over the twenty-plus years he was with the company; those under him lost confidence in his ability to lead and treat them fairly. He lost his friends and completely destroyed morale all in the name of foolish pride.

This is the way it has always been. You have, however, the freedom to move forward. You have the freedom to search out better people and new opportunities and leave people like this to wallow in their own egos. You are nobody's slave. You are a human being and you deserve better. Your life, your thoughts, your efforts are all worth so much more!

Move on. Search for a place where the quantity and quality of your work will define and reward you as you deserve. Work where you can be challenged and appreciated.

Work hard, be thankful, and be humble. Treat your job as if it were a work of art. Look upon it as if it were a gift and everyday an opportunity to serve, learn and grow.

To employers, reward your people with a fair wage. Each week pay them for the good work that they do. Their pay should thank them for their dedication, for bringing skill and diligence to the workplace and for caring about the job at hand. Treat them like people first and employees second.

* * * *

I could talk for hours about missed opportunities and the games that life plays. Like you, I have been adrift on the seas of frustration and disappointment where lost days, lost weeks, lost months and lost years become troubled memories of what could have been.

Determine your own level of compensation!

I craved change and complained about my life, and yet I wouldn't lift a finger to alter my situation. I saw the hills I had to climb before me and wished that someone would carry me to the top. All I ever thought about was what I should have been doing every day but didn't. I waited and hoped and watched time pass me by. But one day, I saw a situation that helped open my eyes.

We all know people who are facing retirement and have very little income to look forward to except a meager pension and what they can manage to put away over the next year or so. Their stories are commonplace. They are in their early sixties. They live in an apartment or, because they have taken out a second or third mortgage over the years, they still have monthly payments and little in the way of equity. They have no savings. No investments exist. No life insurance has been purchased. Life has just seemed to slip by. There is always next year.

One minute they are twenty and have their whole life ahead of them. The next minute they are sixty and scrambling to secure their future. Their neglected bodies yield to the stress of hard work done too late in life and they break down under a crushing burden of debt and anxiousness. It is such an old story.

A little sleep, a little slumber, a little folding of the hands to take life easier and poverty comes upon us like a bandit and scarcity like a thief in the night.

* * * *

The borrower is always servant to the lender no matter what the transaction. Each day we serve the past, the present and the future to our own benefit or our own regret. We either build or we tear down.

Therefore, we must make our days serve us. We must do all the right things in a wise and timely manner and avoid the subtle slavery that has each of us in bondage. We must make life serve us, not the other way around. We must open our eyes, cut the strings, and strive for independence and self-sufficiency. But, where can we start?

We can start anywhere. We can start in a corner of our room. We can clean and arrange it until it shines and move

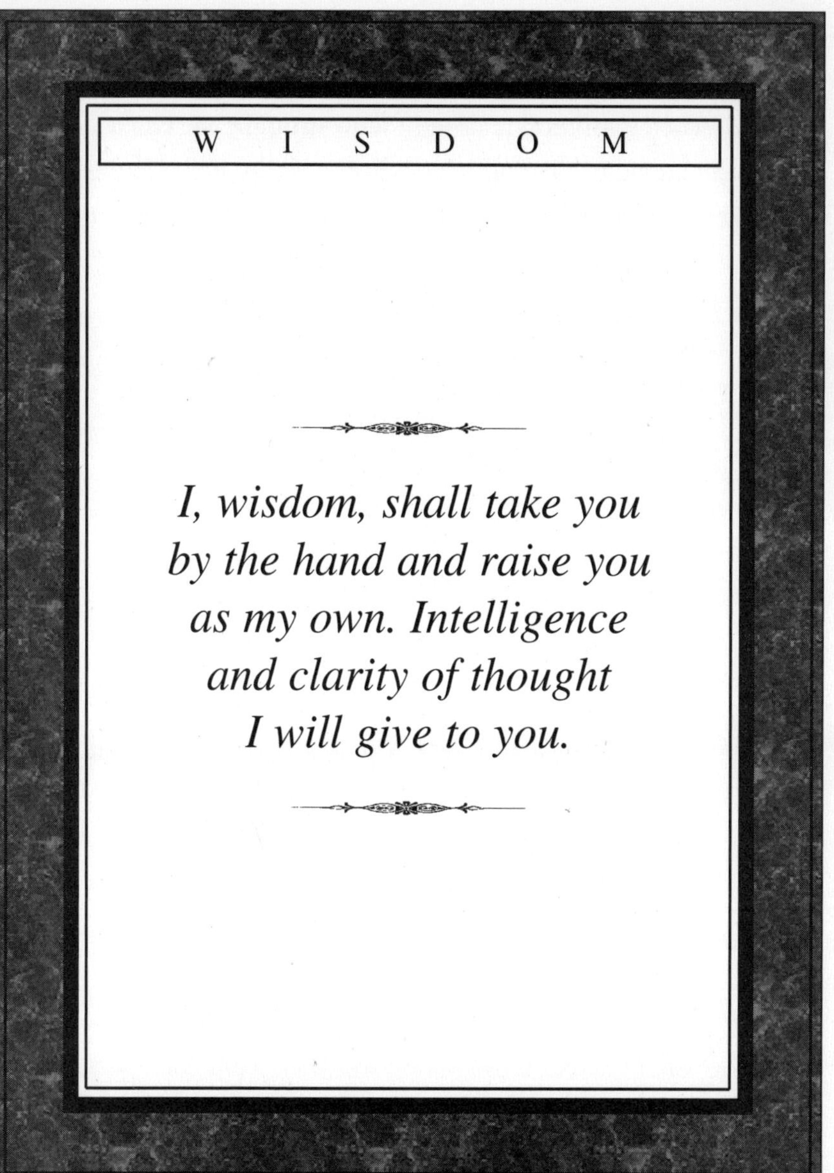
W I S D O M
I, wisdom, shall take you
by the hand and raise you
as my own. Intelligence
and clarity of thought
I will give to you.

on. We can begin a new course of study towards a better future. We can choose a different path and set goals critically and wisely. We can commit to them, demand a new life and make ourselves follow through. We can evolve! And, when evolution is fraught with struggle, we can accept the challenge of discipline and do it anyway, for it is during these moments that we truly grow. Cherish these times; they are a reward unto themselves.

The Tests Of Life

Even the best are tested.

If you can imagine having to stand steadfast against heinous deceptions, the back stabbing betrayal of an old friend, cover-ups and oppressive abuses of power, you can imagine the piece of my life that I had to suffer to bring you the following.

In the soup that is ego, desire and the competition of a chaotic society you will be continually tested with all that you hold dearest for this is where your heart lies. Indeed, when times of trial come despite wise and noble action, know that you are being tested.

Like Job sitting in ashes, we will suffer and how we meet this suffering is the test itself. For the goal of the universe is to determine whether or not the passions of our heart will cause us to turn from God in the fervor and fury of our own faults. If we pass, we enjoy great moments of transfiguration as the power and love of God takes over a part of us that we clutched at with pride and greedy intent.

Turning two talents into four, we are entrusted with virtues of higher value: wisdom, knowledge, understanding, love, discipline, ethics, justice, and leadership. Each strains both body and mind as silver is separated from the dross and our hearts are tested to the breaking point. Scraping at our sores, what is learned during these times of pain are lessons that you would never seek in times of pleasure and are used

W I S D O M

I shall give you the strength of granite mountains. I will give you peace, and your spirit shall blaze like a thousand suns.

in the future to serve in ways unforeseen.

The simple tests are commonplace; some are more subtle. Money, career, sex, and possessions are all prime targets for the unaware.

Regardless of the degree of subtlety, however, the question posed by the test is always, how will these qualities rest in you? Will you be the good steward and use what is at your disposal in the finest of manners or will you lord it over people and become just another tyrant?

How will you use new gifts? How will they affect you? How will they affect your fellow man? Can you be trusted with more? Can you be trusted with the finer points of life? Are you worthy of tougher challenges and situations that require the highest levels of discernment? Will you turn five talents into ten? For if you can't be trusted with little, how can you be trusted with much?

Unsung Greatness

Character is the mirror of the soul.

What you treasure in your life describes you completely. Every word that you say, every priority you display and every decision you make defines who you are. Each reveals how you think, how you live, what you hold most valuable and the state of your character.

By wisdom and the character it serves, true leaders reign and rulers make laws that are just. Love, kindness, fairness, faithfulness and loyalty keep them safe and bring stability to a company or a country. Upon these rocks, their leadership is founded and justice is made secure.

Although this is the way it should be, it is certainly not the way it is. Network news survives on world leaders that lead by corruption, on heads of state that mock the people they were elected to serve, on companies whose only goal is monetary gain and on stories of injustice that wounds the common man. Nothing changes. Despite thousands of years of this repeated history, injustice remains. Why?

You will rarely find anyone who serves justice skillfully, for man knows little of justice and even those in positions of great power are too blinded by their titles and accomplishments to see clearly to the heart of a matter. Their scales are so askew that they rage at honest mistakes while tolerating thieves and blatant lies. While insignificant offense brings the harshest punishment, crime and corrup-

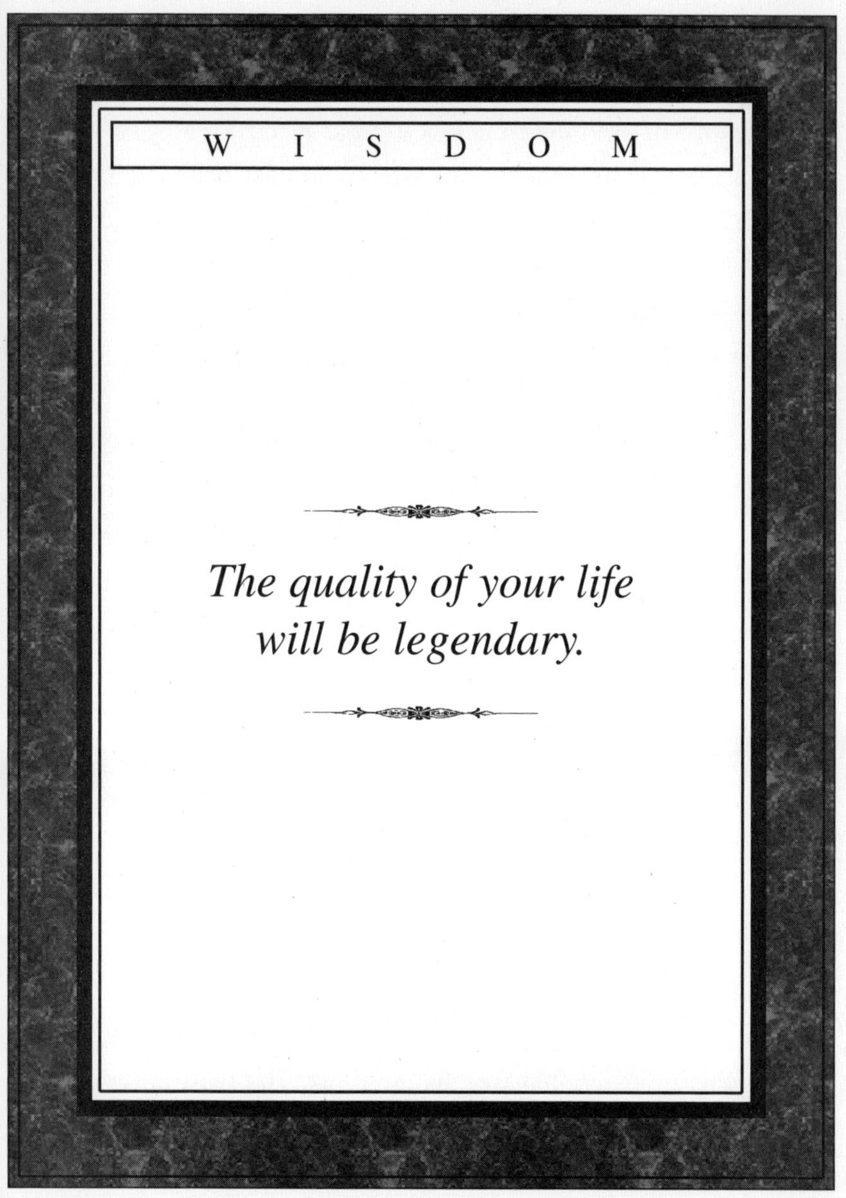

W I S D O M

The quality of your life
will be legendary.

tion are overlooked by blinded eyes.

Their sense of justice is like a tree blowing in the wind; it bends and sways to every breeze be it real or completely imagined. They cannot feel your pain and the significance of your claim is lost in their insensitive eyes.

Naively, it is the way of this world to seek an audience with these people, thinking that this is the way of justice. In fact, nothing could be farther from the truth, because men like these have placed justice into the hands of people who have similar character and now injustice is their collective commerce.

Behind closed doors they take truth and spin it into lies — what once glistened in the sun is tarnished by their tongue. They punish integrity because they cannot recognize it through the haze of their own iniquity and they accept the bribes that put fools into power. Instability and malevolence are the result of all that they touch.

What once glistened in the sun
is tarnished by their tongue.

Everyone has stories about this. I have dozens. The pain comes with the injustice that they impart upon you, and it is this injustice that weighs the most. The frustration lies in our inability to find anyone in authority to see clearly through the lies and apply discipline accordingly. They are blind and deaf and dumb and nothing you could say or do

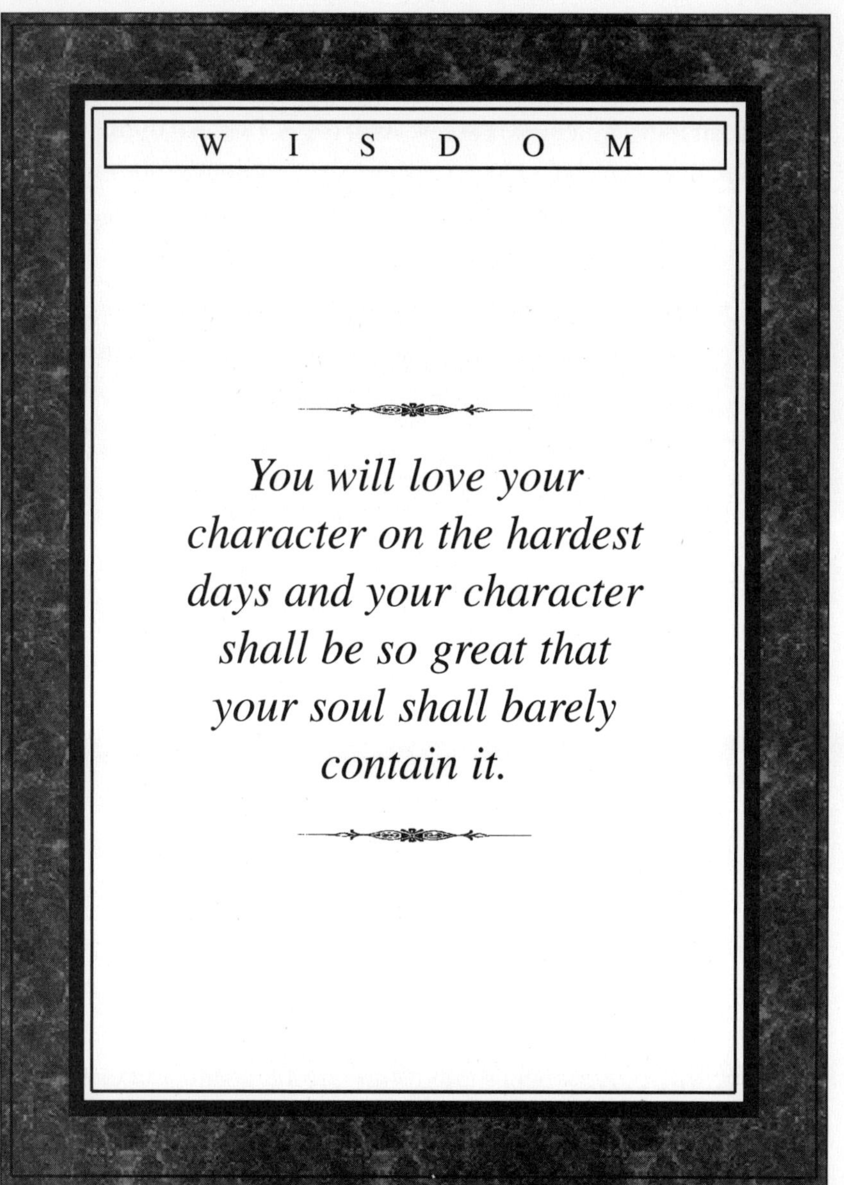
W I S D O M
You will love your character on the hardest days and your character shall be so great that your soul shall barely contain it.

will change them.

* * * *

When a man's power outstrips his wisdom, he becomes dangerous. Decisions are slow in coming because of stubbornness and an inflated sense of self-importance. The decisions that are made are colored with convenience and advantage in mind, and image is protected at all costs. With each opportunity they trade a piece of their character for a piece of power but eventually have neither.

I love the truth of the rose. It looks like a rose, it smells like a rose, it feels like a rose, it lives like a rose and it pricks like a rose. If only people were as simple.

When a true leader sits to judge, he searches out the truth by carefully examining the characters of those before him; for a man of bad character holds justice in contempt and his words cannot be trusted.

True leaders know that people lie. Some people will stand before him and tell him exactly what he wants to hear, some will provide what they think are facts and some will be masters of deception. Everyone has an agenda. So, he looks at their work, their dress, their surroundings, and how they speak to see the hidden heart and hear the muffled mind.

When challenged and pressured, liars huff and puff and feign disdain; whereas the honorable sit like pillars of calm and are willing to state their case at length in the most gentle, genuine and unassuming manner. They know that it takes great strength of character to avoid retaliation so they defuse the moment instead of escalating the emotions. They provide clarity to a problem and give apt solutions. They are concerned about people first and all else second.

I recall an incident where a report was written detailing some very disturbing events and situations that two managers were desperate to cover up. A meeting was called between the CEO, the two managers and the two men who had issued the report.

From the outset, the guilty parties ranted and raved at the CEO, hoping to confuse the issues. The men who wrote the report simply sat and watched them dig the hole deeper.

After they had exhausted themselves, the CEO asked everyone to leave. All left except one of the authors. He waited in silence until the CEO came over to him and asked him why he didn't speak during the meeting. Still he said nothing.

A long minute later, he stood up and looked the CEO straight in the eyes and said simply and calmly, *"Everything in that report is absolutely true."*

The CEO looked at him for a long moment and said, *"I believe you."*

Two weeks later, the senior manager was let go.

W I S D O M
God grants justice in
His own way.
Just give Him time.

How many times have we heard of major criminals receiving minor sentences and minor criminals doing major time? How often have you seen your boss lose it over inconsequential matters while overlooking a serious issue such as sexual harassment?

Once character is established the trial begins.

A proper sense of justice is a skill achieved by those of great character. There is no such thing as a prodigy in this regard. It is learned only with great intent and careful observation; it is born from an appropriate emotional response to the pain of the past and to the sting of injustice.

True leaders understand that what seems trivial to one person may, in fact, be quite traumatic to another. Their heart grows no calluses; what is wrong is plainly seen and their reprimand is carefully weighed.

Discretion lives in them, for it is of highest character to overlook trivial matters. Discipline lives in them, for a glutton and a drunkard will forget what the rules and laws decree and deprive the oppressed of their rights. They refuse to make decisions of convenience or pander to the whims of partiality so that their judgments reveal the true measure of integrity.

In lofty heights where leadership, justice and great character unite, mercy becomes the embodiment of all of

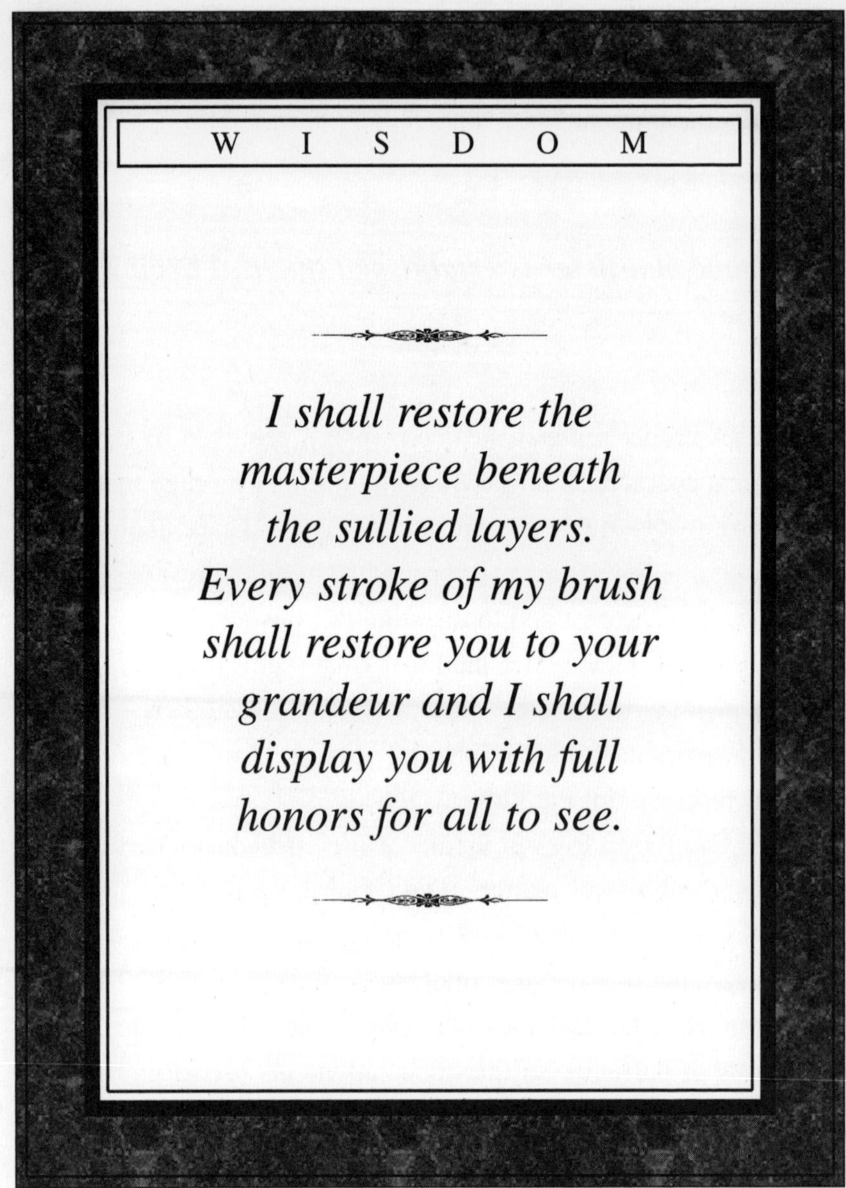
W I S D O M
I shall restore the
masterpiece beneath
the sullied layers.
Every stroke of my brush
shall restore you to your
grandeur and I shall
display you with full
honors for all to see.

the commandments. The uncompromising voice of conscience that whispers to us daily to love our neighbor genuinely, and be generous with time, skills and money is the voice of mercy in action. To grant such mercy is to step above the din, reach out a hand and lift a lost soul from the murky depths of despair.

Life is persuaded with patience.

Cherish the times you can grant mercy, for the opportunities are few yet the reward is extraordinary. Be thankful for the chance to forgive and to bring peace where there is strife. These are the truly important moments of your life. These are the moments that define you and it is here that you are once again revealed. Do not pass them by for they will not come again.

* * * *

See the gentle wind blowing softly through the pines. Feel the tender breeze upon your face. Such a beautiful day, such happiness! To be gentle is the challenge, to be the soft breeze that brings peace to people is the art, and to have a soft tongue that can persuade even the hardest of hearts is the masterpiece.

A patient man has great understanding of the world around him; through patience and persistence anything is possible. This is why the wise are masters of their emotions and their surroundings. As turmoil and confusion build, so too does their calm. They know that there is nothing that requires haste and nothing that haste cannot ruin. They know that only a fool gives full vent to his emotions and composure will win the day.

* * * *

The natural state of the human heart is one of pride and arrogance. Although others may see you as great, you know the truth. You play the game. You don't know what you should know, you don't do what you should do and you are not being who you should be. You revel in your own accomplishments, to your dismay, and suffer the fall that inevitably comes with a mind full of foolishness and a chest swelled with pride.

Our attraction lies in our kindness; our actions merely confirm our love.

To those who seek great character, beware the traps of praise and criticism. They are subtle tests but they never fail to reveal a proud heart. Avoid what is so transparent to others and strive for humility, for only with the humble is wisdom found.

Humility is gentle, kind and patient. It is truth and sincerity, it is love at all times, it is the art of life, and it is God

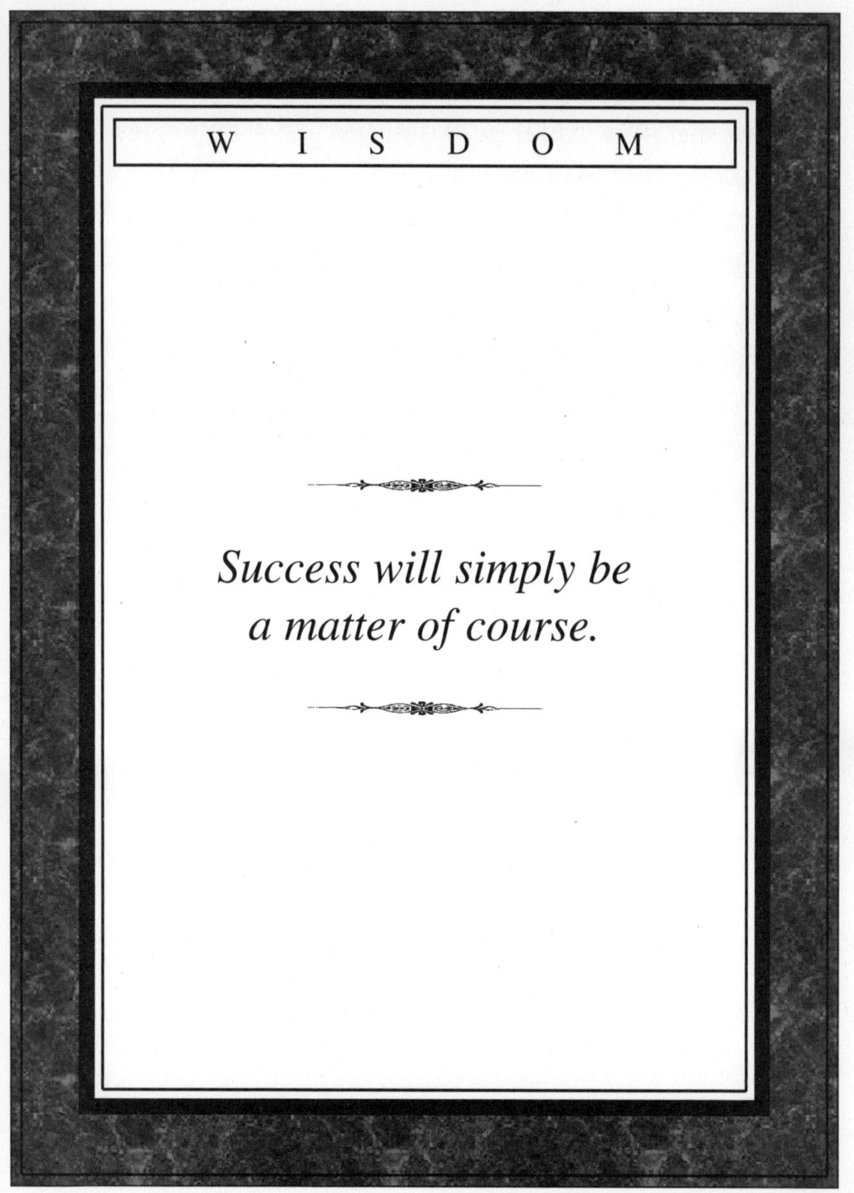
W I S D O M
Success will simply be
a matter of course.

and man in harmony of purpose. Humility comes before honor.

As a worker, become as skilled as you can at what you do. The combination of diligent hands and integrity will result in your being given charge over much. As a leader, be satisfied with your role, live to serve and let your character set you apart. Let love and faith and truth never leave you so that you will win favor and a good name in the sight of God and man.

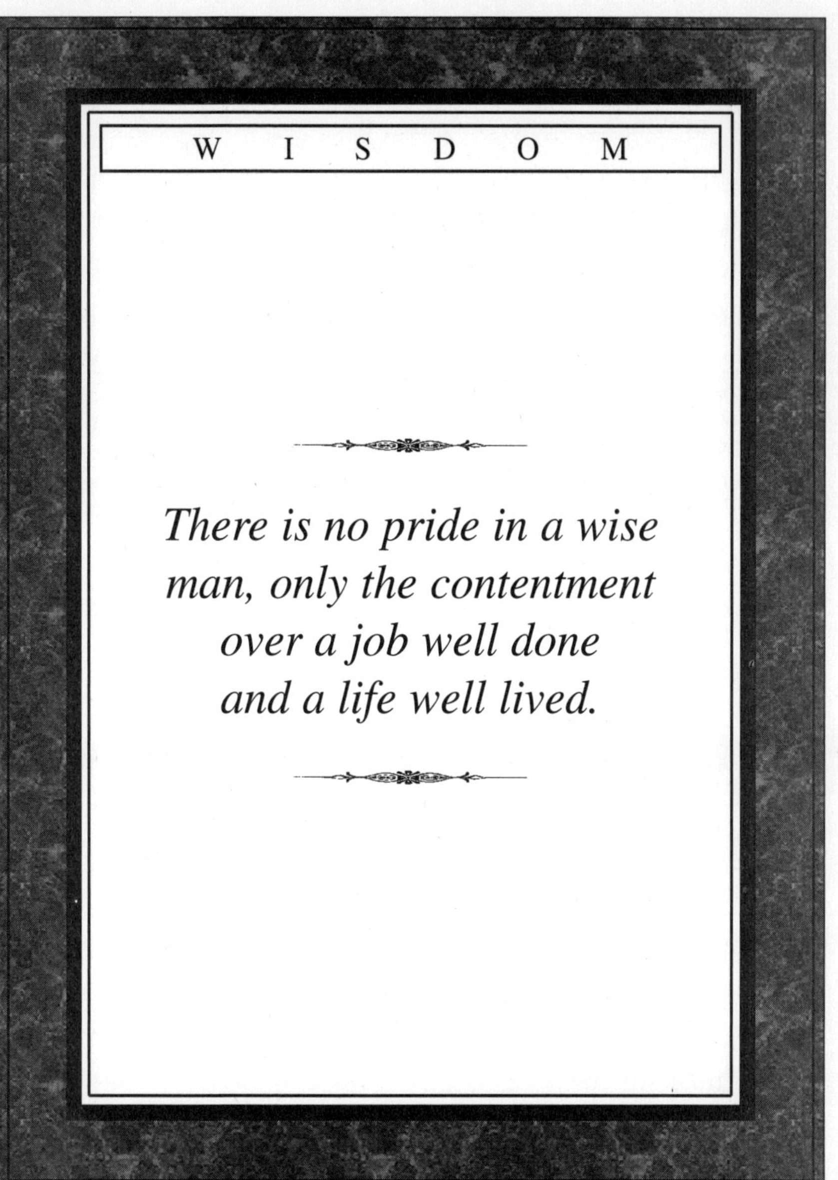

W I S D O M

There is no pride in a wise man, only the contentment over a job well done and a life well lived.

THE FEELING OF CERTAINTY

We are blind by choice.

It never ceases to amaze me that people put so much faith into what they believe to be true, defending it to the last, when in fact their knowledge is clearly flawed and their own insecurity plays plainly across their eyes.

Although all of a man's ways seem right to him, very few truly know anything. Biases color the way we look at everyone and everything. Our decisions are weighed on faulty scales of our own design and we refuse to see the havoc this creates.

A man I knew years ago was caught manipulating hiring policies and was confronted by his supervisor in a very quiet and reserved manner. His supervisor, a good man, was well known for his capacity to see past mistakes and maintain perspective. In fact, all he wanted to do was to remind him of the hiring policies and fix the problems that had been created.

Unfortunately, the fellow refused to admit to any wrongdoing, became enraged at his supervisor and began spouting obscenities. Surprised at the response and shocked at the language, the supervisor sent him back to his office to let him calm down.

The next day, he presented evidence that clearly indicated the breach of protocol and again did so in a gentle and unassuming manner.

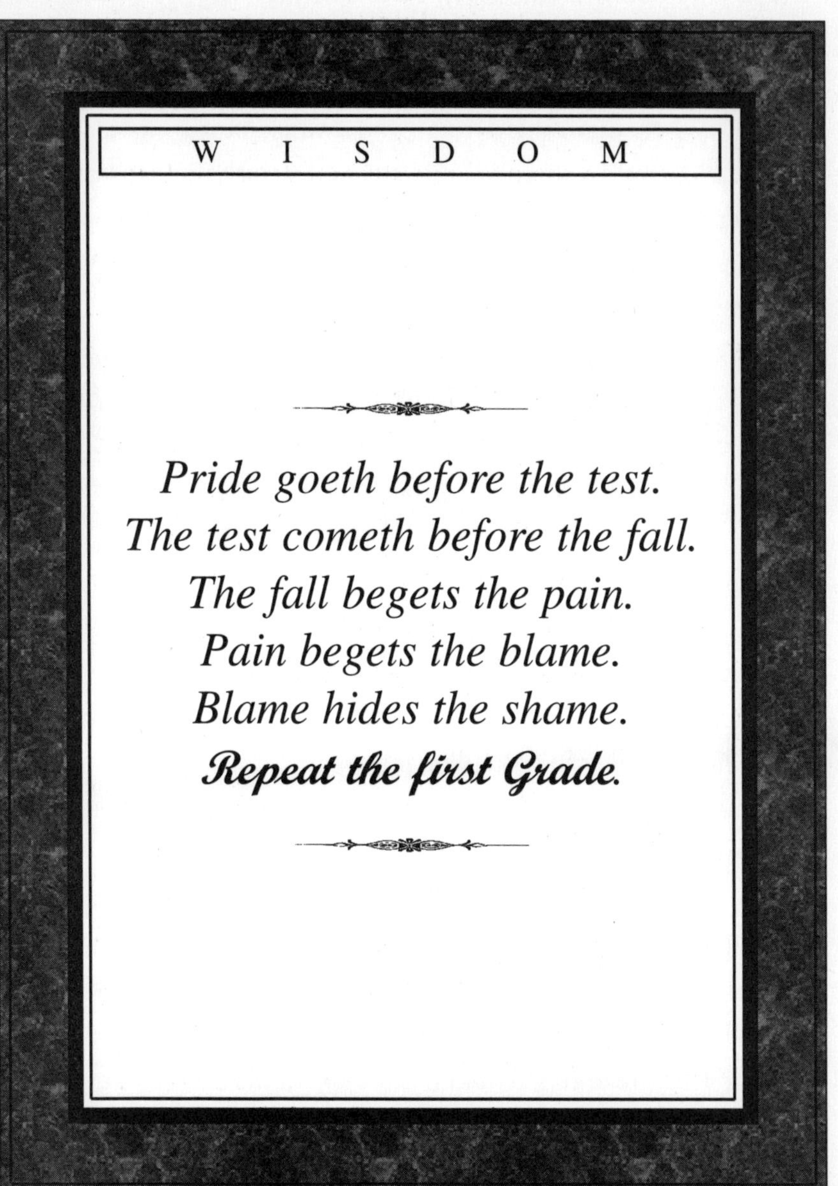
W I S D O M
Pride goeth before the test.
The test cometh before the fall.
The fall begets the pain.
Pain begets the blame.
Blame hides the shame.
Repeat the first Grade.

The man lost his cool again, made more threats, verbally abused him and stormed out of the office. The manager of the department was then informed of the situation and the man's actions.

When confronted for a third time, he just couldn't bring himself to admit his mistake and verbally abused both men. As a result, he was fired from a job that he had worked at for over fifteen years.

Teaching is like a light shining brightly into the darkness of our lives, illuminating all that is wrong and could be right again.

We are blind by choice. We exist on such inaccurate knowledge that our understanding of anything is clouded by the chaos of our own confusion. What we believe to be true is often some assemblage of information obtained through casual conversations and poor recall of information that we didn't learn very well when we had the opportunity.

I remember a young man who thought he knew everything there was to know about his field and regularly took it upon himself to insult and frustrate highly skilled people who had worked in the field for decades.

His coworkers would try to explain the correct way of doing certain tasks but he would have none of it. He would say things like, *"Oh no, you don't understand. This particular case is special."* Or he would say, *"You just let me take care of it. I know the system."*

The disturbing thing about it was that you could see in his eyes that he was desperately trying to cover his lack of knowledge. You could see him mentally searching and hiding, bobbing and weaving. It was tragic.

And then there are the stubborn people who push away the very thing that could help them. *How dare you question me*, they say with their eyes. *I have been doing this all of my life. I know all there is to know and there is nothing you can tell me that I don't already know.*

It is tragic to see people so full of pride that they think they know everything, for they have far too much skill in their own eyes. They are never open to suggestions - never open to negotiation. Their insisting on their own ways despite plain evidence to the contrary destroys their lives.

An engineering friend of mine was working on a particular project that seemed perfect for a new and promising technology he had investigated. Meticulously doing his research and calculating the return on investment, it became clear that replacing the old system with the new equipment would save the company hundreds of thousands of dollars. Management was delighted.

Unfortunately, a particularly difficult man who had been in charge of the system for twenty five years and had little more than rudimentary knowledge of its inner workings, stubbornly refused to see the benefits and flatly dismissed the recommendation. He then spent two months gathering data and traveling to various sites on company time to refute the information that the engineer had put forth. He tried everything, he called everyone, and despite all evidence to the contrary, he stubbornly insisted on the old system. To his humiliation, the new system went in anyway and worked even better than expected.

People like this can be both frustrating and dangerous. Often times their pride and stubborn arrogance causes disturbing results. In most cases, misinformation and abuse occur on a daily basis. Money is lost, employees are frustrated, and careers are hindered. In the extreme, people are injured and die.

To learn, you must be willing to listen.

If only they could see how teaching is like a light, shining brightly into the darkness of their lives, illuminating all that is wrong and could be right again. If only they could see where they have been and see where their ways are taking them, then they could begin to overcome one of life's greatest hurdles.

As individuals, we must obtain information from accurate sources and be constantly looking for new ideas that can build a bridge from where we are today to where we want to be. Only a fool would dismiss the opportunity to learn all that he can. Why would anyone purposely turn away from a world of new and exciting information that could help him become the person he always wanted to be?

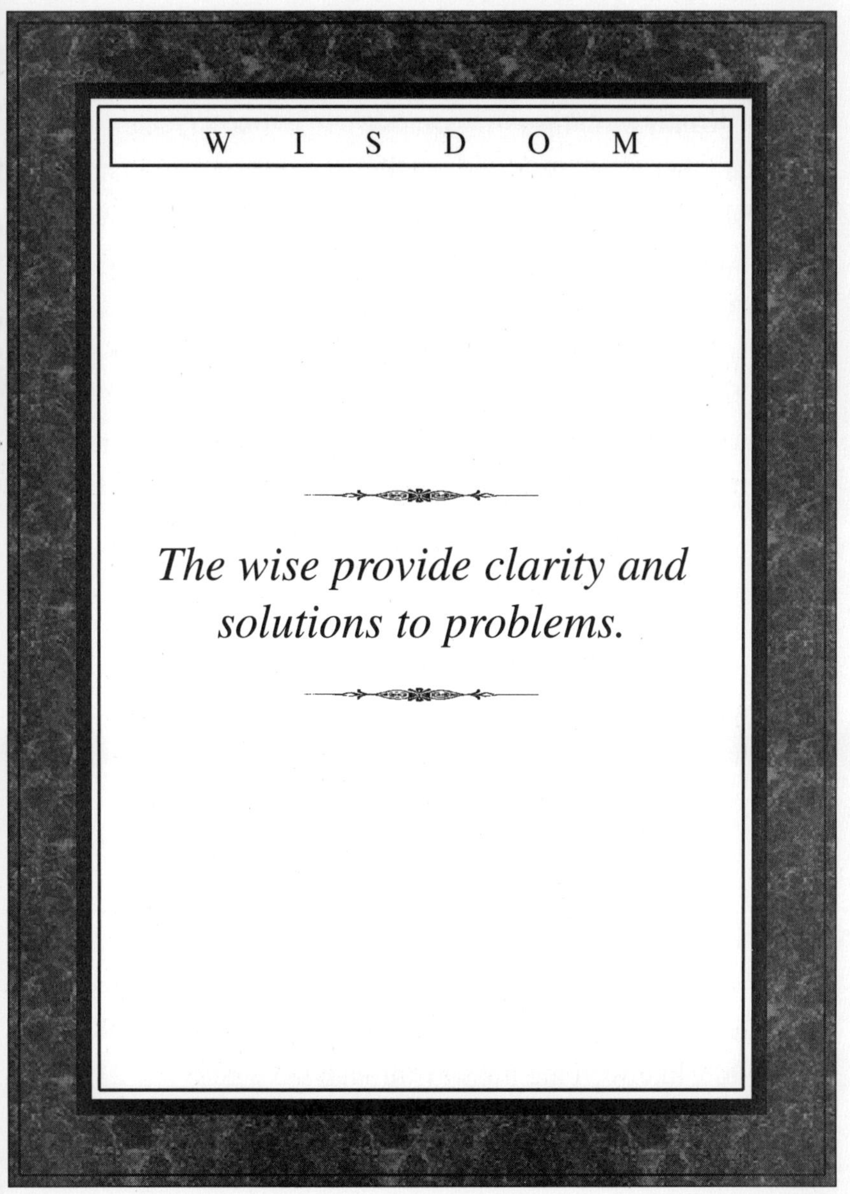

W I S D O M

The wise provide clarity and solutions to problems.

To live like this is to court disaster. The world will take advantage of your ignorance, strangers will invariably feed on your wealth and all of your hard work will go to enrich another.

Understanding is uncommon. It is like crystal clear waters that wash away the confusing mud from your eyes. It is like standing inside truth. To begin to understand is to first say 'I do not know'. Only then will you be ready to learn.

Be careful from whom you learn, for the truly knowledgeable are few and far between. Cautiously balance the selection of your teachers with an understanding of human frailty; even the best of men are prone to errors. If you toss aside every apple you find that has a flaw, you will eventually go hungry.

Those who are wise rarely say anything and what they do say holds great meaning. Although they may have decades of experience, they understand the limits of their knowledge. They are always open to new possibilities and they are always searching for a better way.

At a party one mid-summer's night, I wandered over to a table and sat amidst a group of strangers. They were all talking about the value of knowledge and I became intrigued. At the height of the conversation, one older gentleman told us a story about a meeting he was invited to attend while working his way through university.

As a young man, he sat off to the side in a smoke-filled room as a dozen experts argued about a particularly difficult topic. After listening patiently to impulsive ideas

WISDOM
Genius is found in the silence.

that crashed against egos and obstinacy for the better part of half an hour, the oldest member of the group motioned that he would like to say a few words. The room, acknowledging his years, settled down. Looking at no one in particular, he leaned forward, spoke one sentence and sat back in his chair. Stunned, his listeners shook their heads in amazement as his one simple sentence clarified the problem and solved it at the same time. Having been touched by wisdom, the meeting ended in murmurs of awe and silent admiration.

I read it and thought I knew it; I didn't.
I wrote about it and thought I knew it; I didn't.
I lived it and thought I knew it; I didn't.
I felt the lessons burn my soul and
now I truly know.

Wise people truly are remarkable. Observing them, you will find that they are patient when they teach, and their correction is gentle when you make a mistake. They listen, and freely admit when they do not know. They will tell you that truth and wisdom are found only in the discernment of details, several layers beneath erroneous assumptions and a world of laziness and deception.

They will also tell you that you should accept correction with great humility, for it truly is a gift. Correction allows you to see past your flaws and reminds you of the inescapable truth that, even though you may have years of

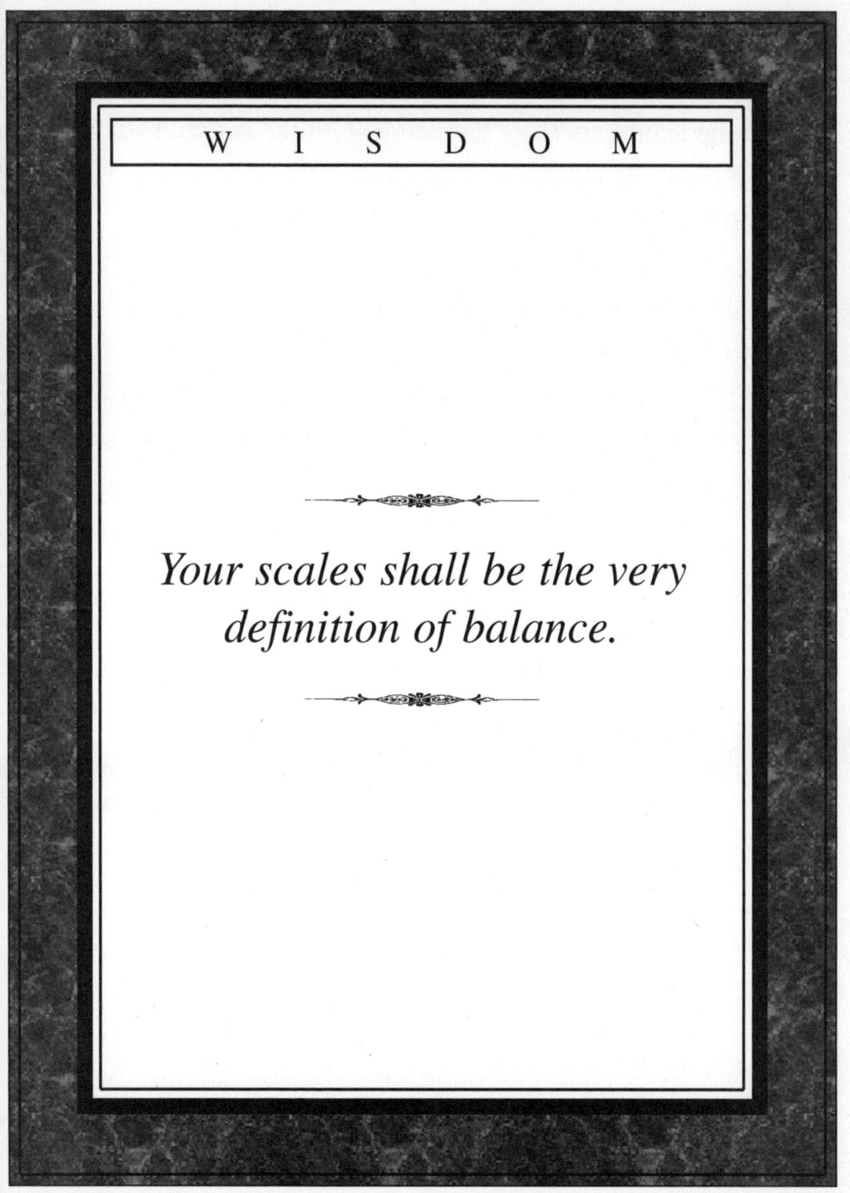
W I S D O M
Your scales shall be the very definition of balance.

experience and your knowledge strains to burst forth from the seams of your intellectual pride, you don't know everything.

Thus, you will be taught to make no rash decisions in times of stress — to slow down and think clearly, weighing your plans in consultation with experts, getting the right information; getting accurate information.

You will find that they are silent when they are being scolded; they are silent when they are being praised. Therefore, you too will learn to be silent, hold your words and learn.

You will be taught to think clearly about what is being said, about the logic and about the truth; to weigh things with wisdom in mind and ultimately to make wise decisions a habit.

Lastly, they will teach you the value of the past: to appreciate all the sacrifices that have been made to make your world more livable and to do your part to contribute to the whole.

If you find wise people, cherish your time with them. They are good people and they are rare people and they truly are few and far between.

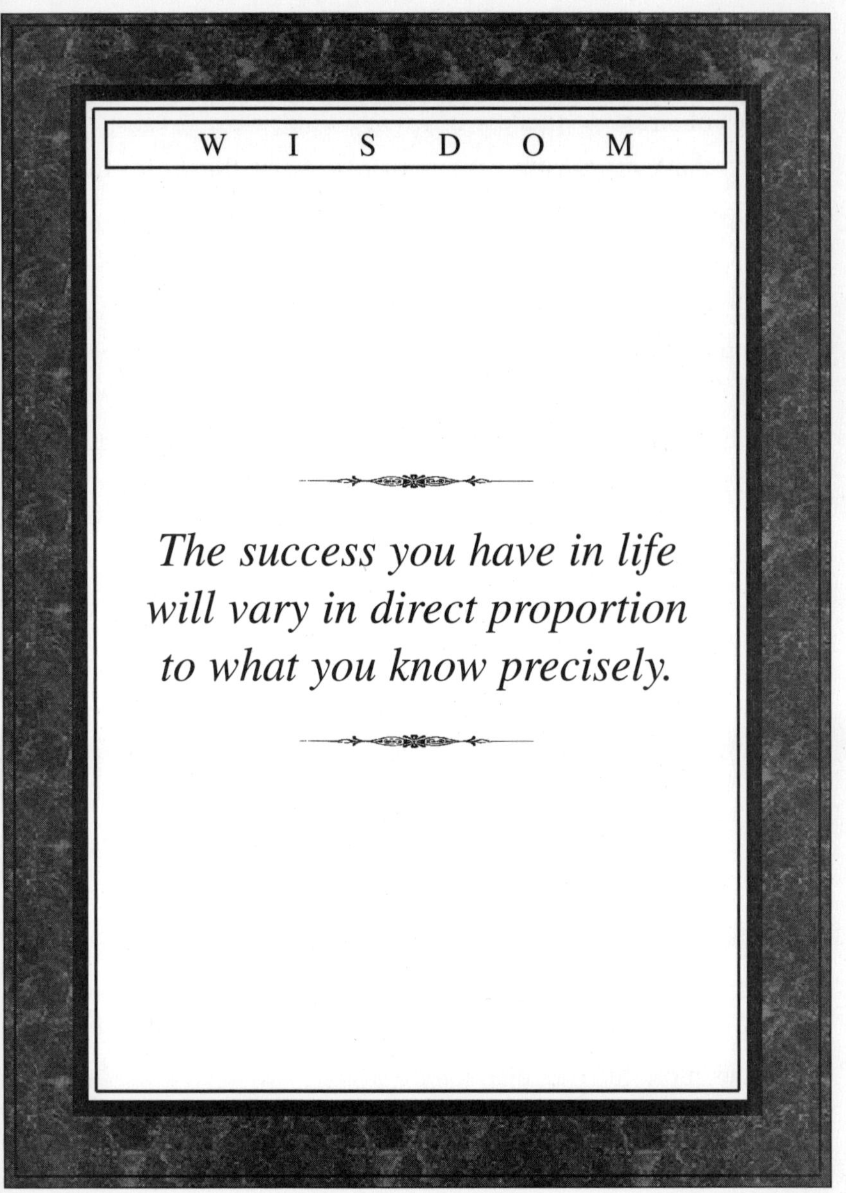

W I S D O M

The success you have in life will vary in direct proportion to what you know precisely.

Deafening Silence

What is in the heart is revealed by our words.

We live and die by our words. From the fruit of our lips we prosper as surely as the work of our hands rewards us.

Like ripples in a pond, what we say and do propagates throughout our lives. The words that we speak, read, write and think are the beds that we make for ourselves. Every word that we mutter builds upon the last. They either tear us down or build us up.

Hold your plans in your heart.
This world has ears and there are many
who will tear down what you wish to build up.

I met a man who had just been hired into a position of great power. He was very polite, professional, and was the embodiment of his senior position within the company; yet during our fifteen minute meeting, he spoke one seemingly insignificant sentence that told me everything I needed to know about his true character.

After the meeting, I cautioned those who would be dealing with him to consider a specific course of action before he could derail a major project that would require his

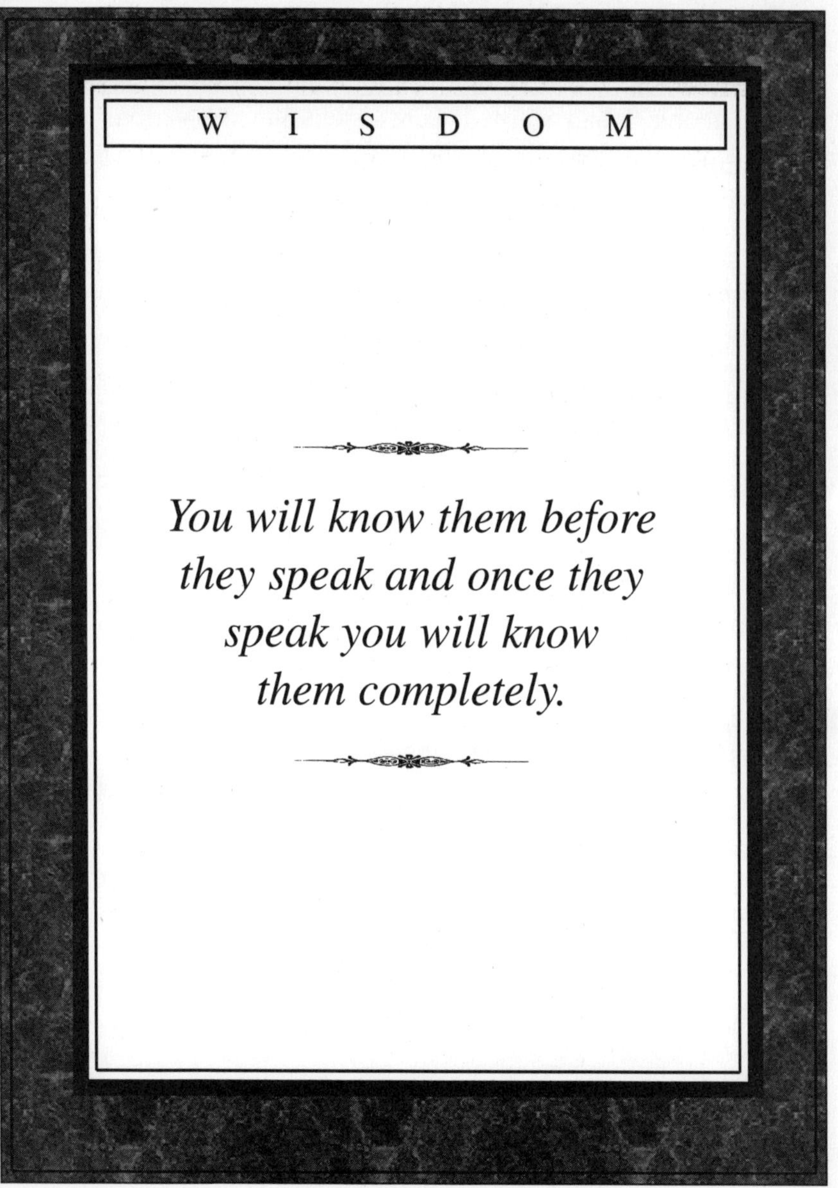

W I S D O M

You will know them before they speak and once they speak you will know them completely.

collaboration. Unfortunately, my suggestion was met with skepticism. After all, he had just been hired based on excellent credentials.

A few months later, my suspicions were confirmed as the people I had warned were discussing the serious and disturbing problems he was creating.

True beauty lies in the wisdom of the soul and with words it is revealed.

If you must talk, be discrete, and think many times before saying anything. Realize that your words will rarely make a difference so sit in silence and be patient. Refuse to play the part of the fool and leave the stage for others to struggle upon. Remember your place and hold your tongue.

I can't tell you how many times I have avoided confrontations and arguments, that would only have led to discontent and bad feelings, by not saying anything. The words directed at me are offensive, the emotions have been summoned and everything inside of me is rebelling at how I am being mistreated.

But what is required at these times is perspective and focus. Before me lie an infinite number of paths that I may take, as my choice of words and how I might say them arouse uncomfortable possibilities. Consequences strain the evolution of the moment.

Although cancer, war, starvation and poverty are real

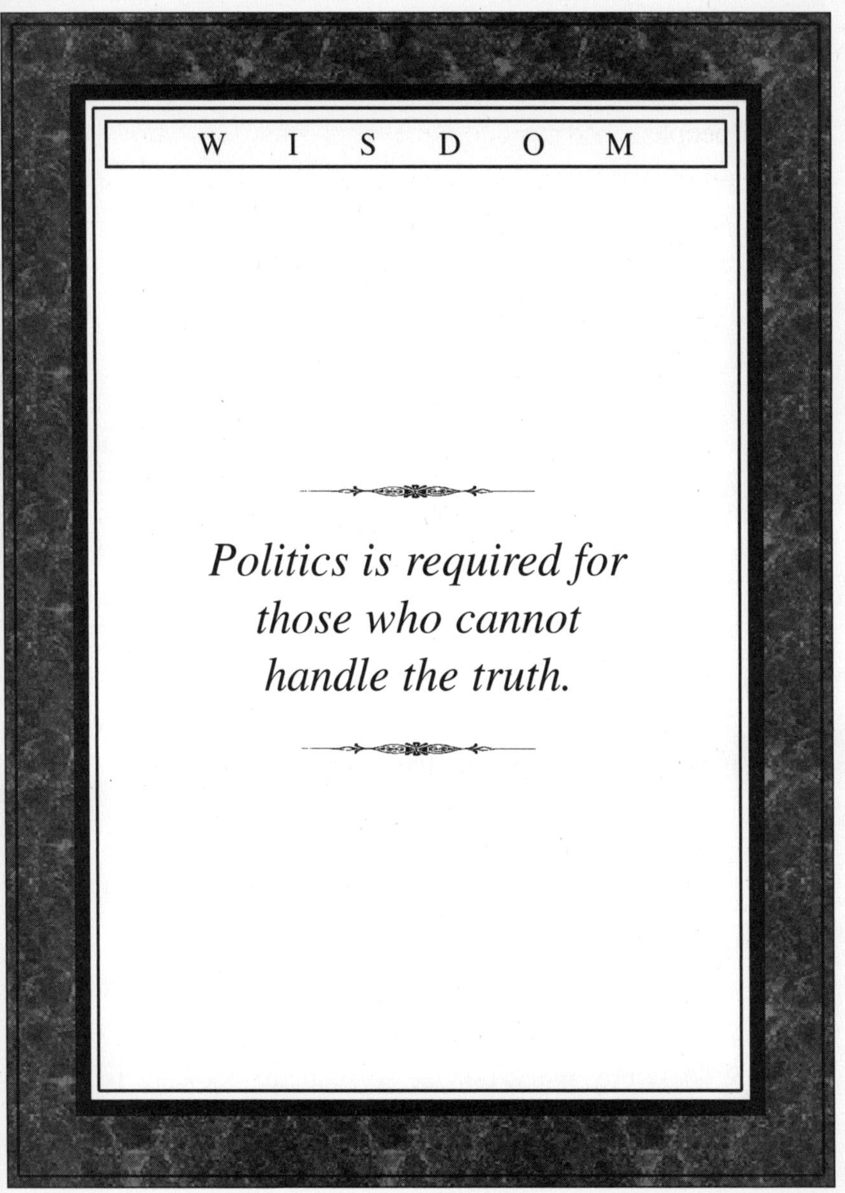
W I S D O M
Politics is required for those who cannot handle the truth.

problems that justify strong words, actions and emotions, to me this verbal barrage is nothing but a gift of perspective that reminds me of the blessings that I have to be grateful for and insight into a dishonorable character for future reference.

Do not mistake politeness for sincerity.
Do not confuse credentials with character.

My choice is silence and wisdom wins again. The only price to be paid is to my ego and it is a small price to pay for the peace that comes from appeasing the moment.

* * * *

We can be a cruel and heartless species. The weak are mocked by the strong, the slow are teased by the intelligent, the poor are snubbed by the rich and tragedy is packaged in videos for amusement.

What is learned later in life, however, is that even the strong become old and decrepit, the intelligent lose their faculties, the rich can lose their wealth overnight and you too can be on a video one day. Mockery is a recipe for disaster; this planet will respond.

Therefore, mock no one so that life does not mock you. Do not scoff at, mimic, tease or treat anyone with scorn, ridicule, or contempt. You do not know their pain nor their history.

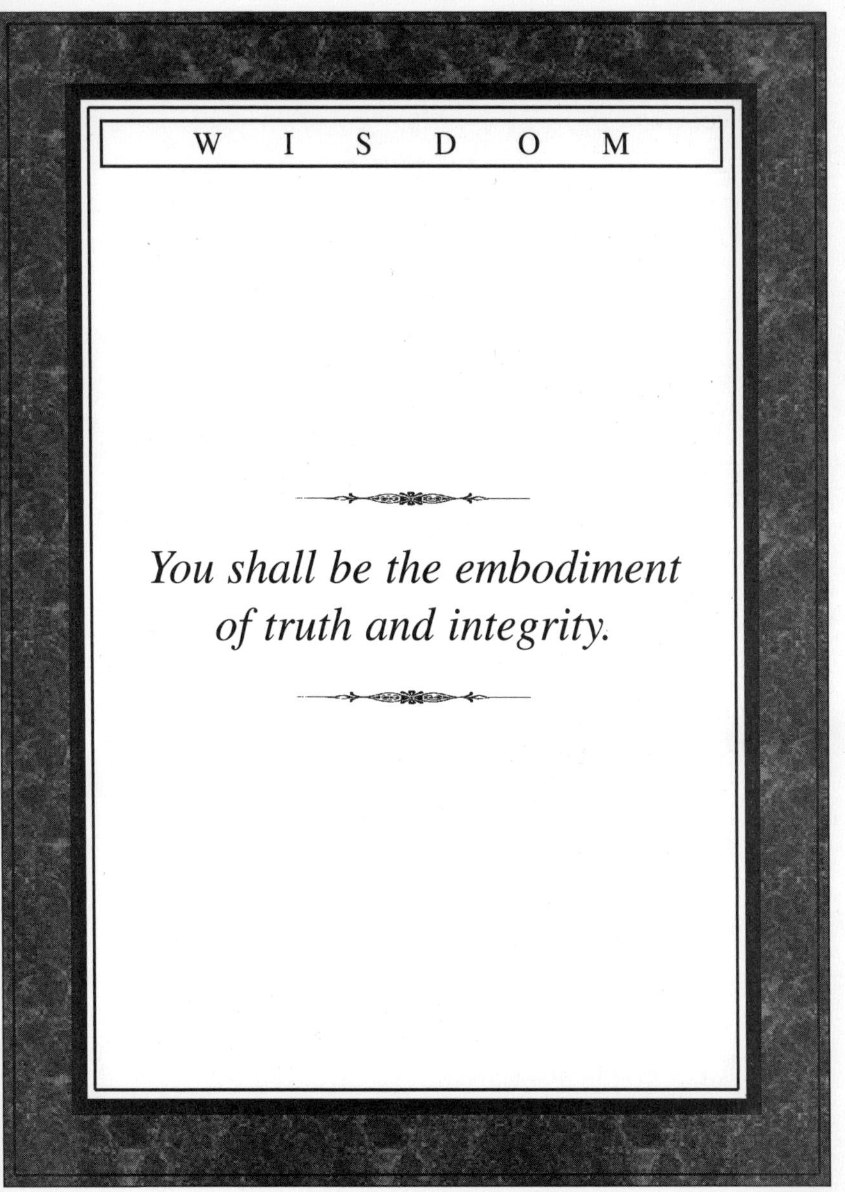

W I S D O M

You shall be the embodiment of truth and integrity.

Never mock the poor, the lowly, or the destitute lest you find yourself on the same paths and all hope is lost. Never gloat over disaster. Understanding the cards that some are dealt is wisdom in this regard.

Discretion shall live in you.

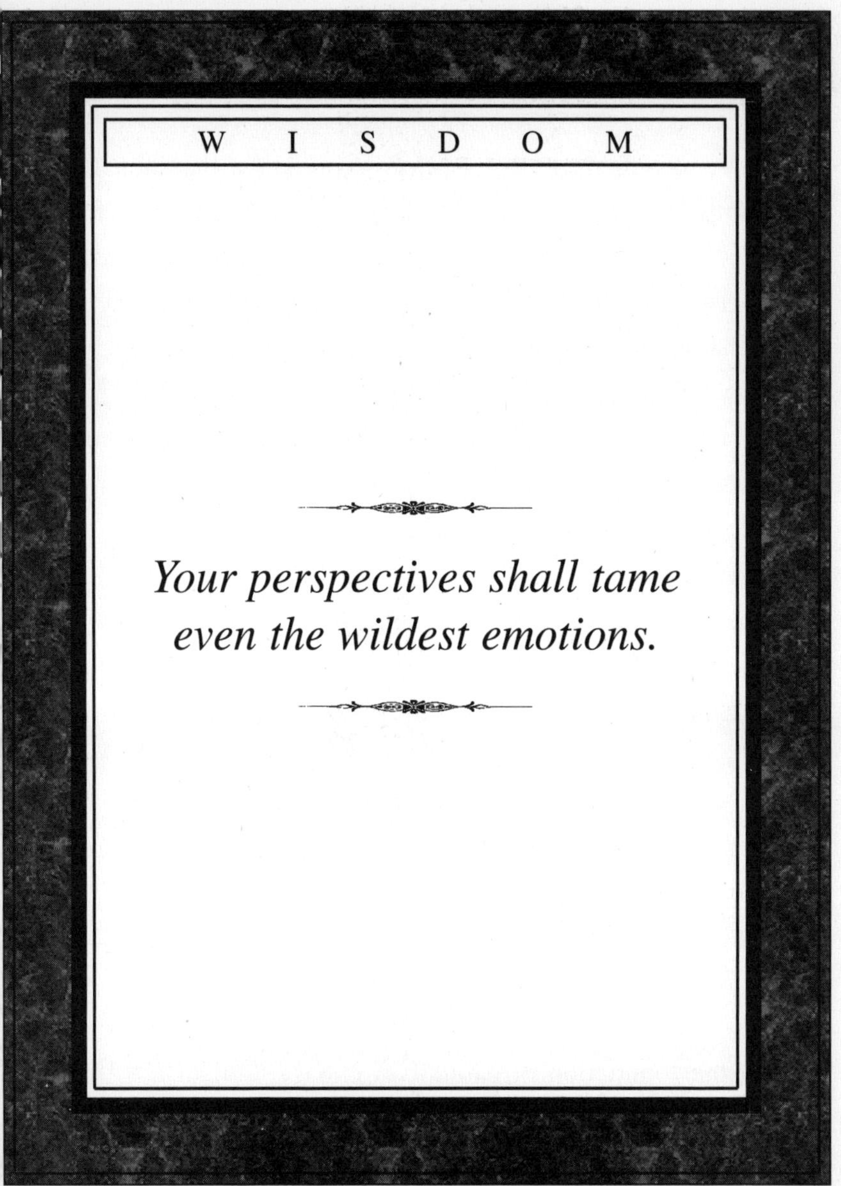

W I S D O M

Your perspectives shall tame even the wildest emotions.

Just Rewards

The borrower will always be slave to the lender.

I have had my fill of poverty and know the value that struggling people place on a dollar. For some, it is all they have. It has been hard-earned and is fraught with anxiety because there are none left in the pockets and very few are on the way.

The bank account is flush with regret about the past, the struggle of the present, sleepless nights and hard, thankless work that is fueled by Kraft dinners and instant coffee. Take a dollar from my hand, and you take a big part of me with it.

I have also experienced times of modest abundance and cringe at the reckless manner in which these dollars were spent. I had no appreciation of what I had given up in exchange for my money. I was blind to the price I was paying, deaf to the struggle inherent in the transaction and dumb to the value I was receiving. In retrospect, my life, my time, and my efforts were worth so much more than a bag of chips and a cheap pair of jeans.

If I could restore the lost ideals of both personal and corporate capitalism, I would do so by reminding the world that the foundation of capitalism is basic human need and not profit for profit's sake.

An exchange should be made with respect for the fundamental needs of a person and reverence for the currency that is being offered. Profit should be a recognition of the time and skill involved in the product or service and the payment should be received knowing that it represents someone's time and personal effort be it as mighty or meek as it may. Therefore, each exchange should be met with a willingness to serve with skill and dignity, taking only enough to satisfy the investment and secure a modest household. There is no justification for greed.

Poverty in all of its forms is shunned. We close our eyes to those in need and we blind ourselves to our own inadequacies. Just as we step over the destitute on the street, we avoid dealing with our own shortfalls and use the square peg of internal rationalization to deal with the holes our decisions leave behind.

Without wisdom, we are the impoverished.
Without wisdom, we become the oppressed.

Poverty begets pain and pain is an easy target for the arrows of manipulation and mockery. On the plains of life, weaknesses are exploited. People make their living from other people's pain by plundering the depths of suffering. Thus, great prosperity for one usually comes at great cost for many. It is shameful, but it is the way it has always been.

True prosperity is born from understanding poverty in all of its forms. It goes far beyond the financial. Prosperity of any kind, be it health, love, family, etc., is the result of

W I S D O M
Vanity lives in the big house;
prosperity with the meek.

cultivating our lives, our talents and our opportunities while striving for self-sufficiency and the betterment of mankind.

Just as one wise person cannot change the world, being wise in only one small area of your life will not change your circumstances.

Prosperity in any endeavor comes as a result of applied wisdom and generosity; for only with wisdom come the riches, honor, and the enduring wealth we so desire.

What applies to money applies to friends. If I have no friends, I have squandered my relationships. What applies to money applies to the spirit. If my eyes see only darkness, it is because I have avoided the light. What applies to money applies to society. If we suffer collectively, is it not due to a lack of wisdom on the whole?

Pleasure is our downfall. Lack of discipline destroys us. We succumb to the easy way, the unhealthy way, the immoral way, and the foolish way. Every poor decision becomes a loan that gives us a moment's worth of ease and pleasure but is paid back with the stress and strain of an uncertain future. To be wise is to live with this understanding and do the right thing despite the extra effort. To be wise is to be a good steward in all aspects of our lives.

Financially, only wisdom can produce sustainable wealth and a peaceful mind at the same time. Only the dis-

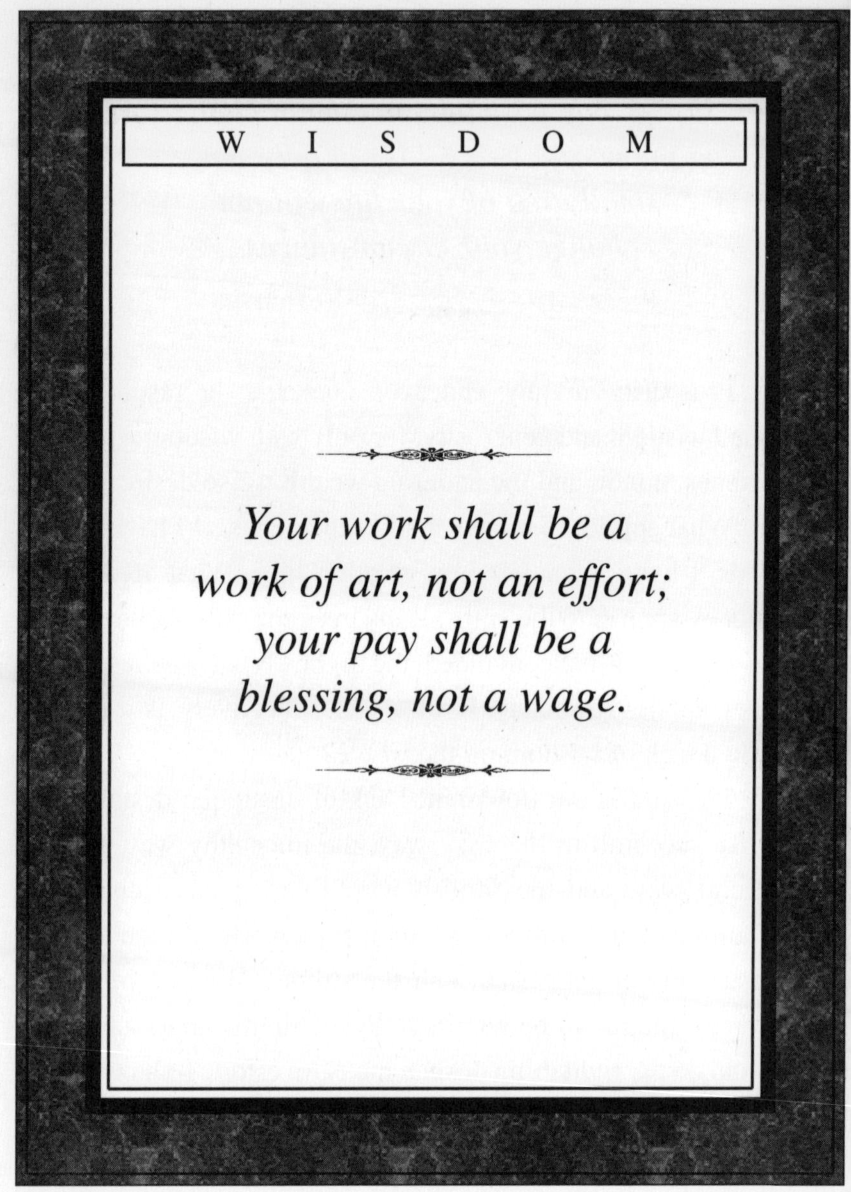
W I S D O M
Your work shall be a
work of art, not an effort;
your pay shall be a
blessing, not a wage.

ciplined and diligent are richly blessed in such a manner.

True wealth is accumulated by careful spending and investing. Those who carefully cultivate what they have and do not waste their resources on undue pleasure grow rich slowly and steadily. All other paths are designed to part the fool from his money.

The ideals of capitalism that are service and quality have been violated. Instead of building value and vision, our marketplace caters to greed and takes pride in useless products.

To have abundance, plan: get the best workers and the best teachers, use the best seed, care for your fields, and harvest in a timely fashion lest the weather changes and injustice steals away what you have worked so hard to grow. Ration: an indulgence today can sacrifice a harvest that could have fed your family an entire winter.

* * * *

It is not a sin to be wealthy, but few people are capable of bearing the burdens and passing the tests that come with it. In times of prosperity, we begin to think that our wealth is our fortress; when, in fact, our riches ransom our time and energy and become the crucible in which our character is tested. We become arrogant and forget our humble

W I S D O M

I own nothing.
The leaves are not the tree.

beginnings. We think ourselves accomplished and mistake this for wisdom. In our pride we speak harshly to others and look down our noses at the poor and destitute. In time, we lose our self and become slaves to our wealth.

It is a tragic and very wide road. It is tragic how we wear ourselves out to get rich. We sacrifice all that is truly important for that which is least important, giving us a plate that is full yet barren of food.

If you do become rich, remember to live well below your means and do not put on airs, because a man who puts all of his faith in his wealth will surely fall, and the wealth that he is most proud of will be taken away to remind him of humility. A man need only remember that rich or poor, the Lord is the maker of them all.

Unite mercy and generosity. To those who have, more will be given, and to those who don't have, even what they have will be taken away.

To become self-sufficient should be your goal. To attain this position, you must be wise and know the state of your affairs thoroughly. Let your investments grow steadily and safely. Do your homework, be prudent and be diverse.

Avoid partnerships. Do not back an investment that could leave you holding debt because of poor judgment on the part of another investor. If he lacks the means to pay, you may lose everything you have and your assets will go

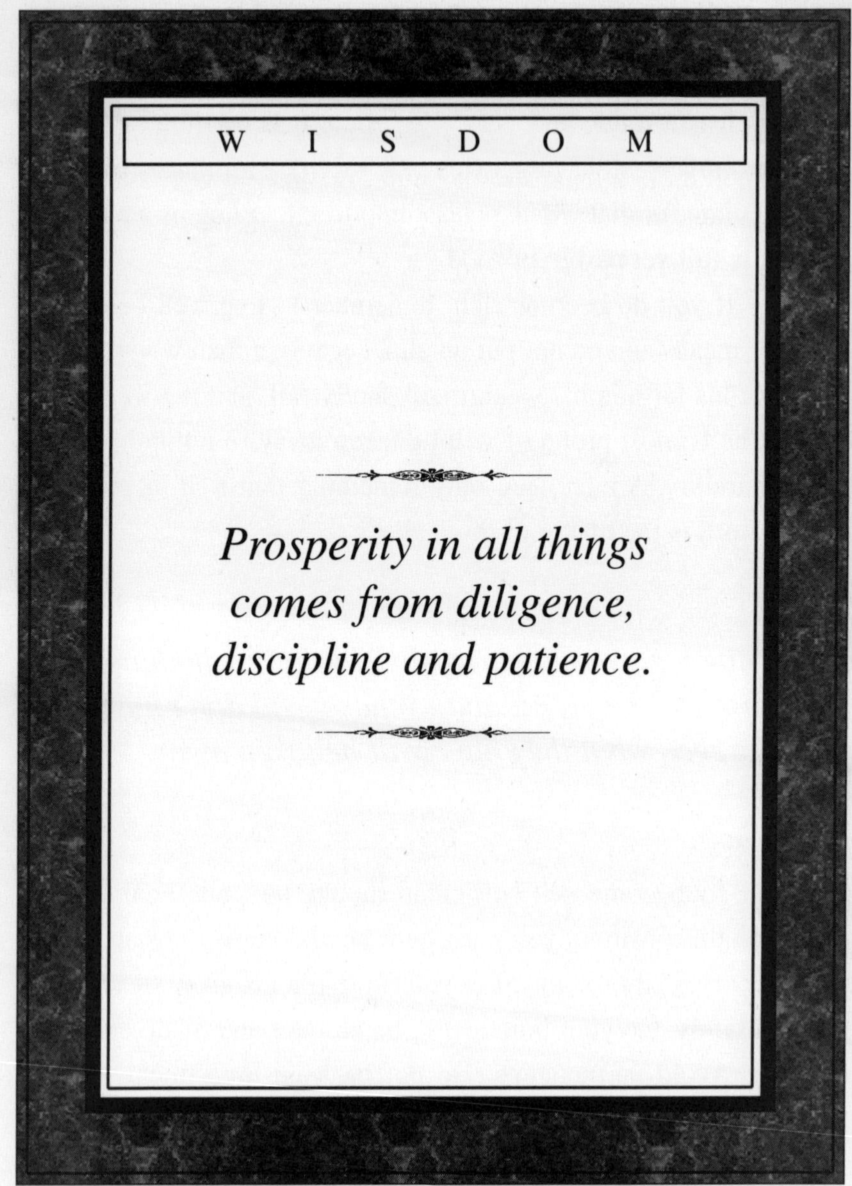
W I S D O M
Prosperity in all things comes from diligence, discipline and patience.

to profit persons unknown.

Lastly, remember that your life is counted only in days. Therefore, tread lightly. Strive for simplicity and balance lest you become a slave to your excesses and ransom your days. Make every decision, great or small, something that will build a magnificent future. Do unto your life as if it were a masterpiece and it will reward you with all that is great and wonderful.

RELATIONS

I wish that I were a better man.

I have seen the road that leads to the destruction of marriages. I know why other people become so tempting; the eyes wander and the heart remembers.

We ache. We ache for the days when our bodies and minds were free to explore each other in passion and love. We miss the sights, the sounds and the touches that told us we were alive. We want to be eighteen again and kiss each other as if we had never kissed before — to burn with desire so hot that we can barely contain our souls. We desperately want the unbridled passion of our youth and it takes all of the discipline within us to hold each other alone in our gaze.

There is so much that we miss, and the paths of desire that lead us into another's arms are all too subtle. Though we stand beside the searing flame we ignore the fire because we simply find it too hard to turn away from the allure. Alas, our will is the weakest when the temptation is the greatest.

Yet, we must never be unfaithful. At all costs, we must remember the covenant of marriage that we made before God. To do otherwise is to choose a bloodied road, choked with the thorns of consequence that will tear precious family and irretrievable love from our flesh.

Write your vows in pillars of granite and honor the sacred covenant between a man and a woman. Let your love be for your spouse alone.

W I S D O M

Imagine being merciful in unexpected times.

While married, nurture the best parts of one another. Bring honor to your marriage and forever treat the other as sacred. Cherish the time that you have with one another and protect each other from the ways of the world. Pray together.

You have been blessed
with souls to care for.

As for children, you do not own them any more than you own the air that you breathe. You have been blessed with souls to care for; into your hands God has commended their spirit. Treat them lovingly, wisely and fairly.

In their youth, there will be times when discipline is the only message that is strong enough for them to hear. Let your correction be carefully applied in timely fashion, however, so that when they are older they will benefit from it. Only then will they will grow up strong and free.

* * * *

Why do we treat dogs better than people? Why do we treat strangers better than we treat our own family? Why do we shun the poor and favor the rich? Most who have cut a swath through humanity and now breathe the thin air of great riches have done so by force and justify their actions as common business practice. As human beings, they are far

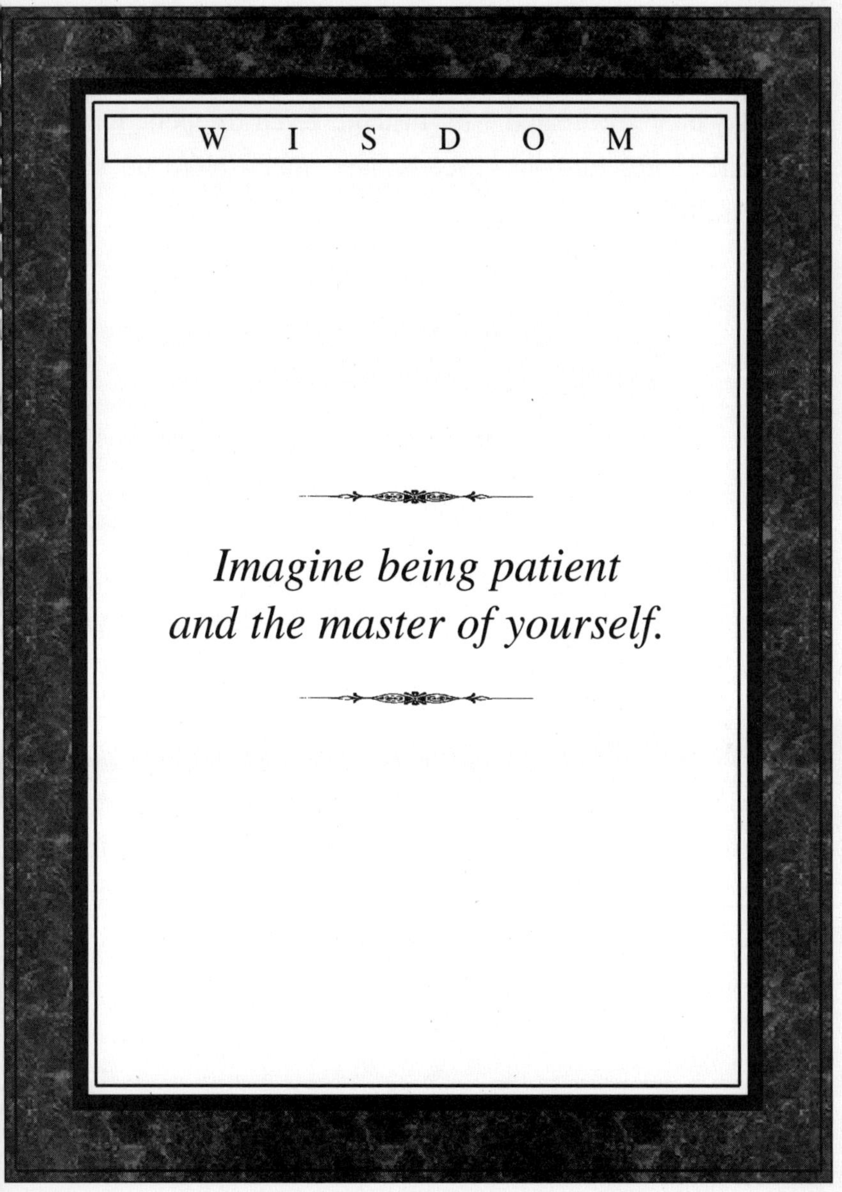
W I S D O M
Imagine being patient
and the master of yourself.

from exemplary and yet we treat them as if they were elite and their accomplishments worthy of praise.

In disturbing contrast, the poorest of the poor can be saintly and be of the finest character and yet to our own discredit they are treated with disdain. Even the poor man's brother hates him, his friends, how much more do they desert him!

To forgive someone is to
acknowledge the divine within you.

Regardless of opinion, until your own life is perfect, do not judge another; for how you judge, you too shall be judged. Should your neighbor need clothing, understand that few are wise with their money and life can be hard. Be compassionate and give him your coat. Should your neighbor need food, understand that few are wise and life can be harsh. Be merciful and give him your food. If they are in prison, know that few are wise, be sympathetic and lend him your ear. If they are ill, understand that few are wise, be empathetic and give them kind words to soothe and heal them.

WISDOM
Imagine being humble.

The third hardest thing to do in life is to conceal a matter in the interest of peace. To overlook an insult is true strength. To avoid strife is to honor yourself and those around you.

The second hardest thing to do in life is to forgive someone. We have been conditioned to be intolerant of one another's failings and yet so accepting of our own. We cringe at boasting but boast ourselves. We are shocked by liars yet lie ourselves. Forgive people, for you do not know the pain in their lives nor the past that creases their brow. In truth, we all lack wisdom in its many forms and those around us struggle just as we do.

The hardest thing to do in life is to forgive ourselves. We cannot run away from the truth that is our past and present but we can change the future. We can be our own best friend. We can be impartial about who we are, and in the quiet times we spend alone, we can be blunt and accepting. We can be strong enough to change the parts of us that need changing and become the person we were always meant to be. We can work hard on our weaknesses. We can strive, and forgive and we can love the person we are becoming.

* * * *

While you live, be gentle in your dealings, be kind of heart and gracious of speech. Be careful with your words and your responses. Say only what you know to be true and accurate. Avoid gossip and be quick to overlook an offense. Doing these simple things will save many relationships.

W I S D O M
Imagine having a great and noble character.

Nevertheless, be cautious. Although you may have a friend who will tell you the truth and who seems to love you at all times, most people are but a single word or action away from deserting you.

In your dealings with your fellow man, let history be your guide:

- *Do not accuse anyone without reason. Do not give false testimony for this will only breed evil.*
- *Do not mock, scoff at or deride anyone.*
- *Do not forsake your friends.*
- *Do not plot harm against your neighbors. Avoid them if they are disagreeable.*
- *Do not get caught up in the foolishness of others - it is a snare and a very old story.*
- *Avoid violent or wicked men, for they will lead you down dark paths.*
- *Be wary of the hot-tempered men. Do not associate with one easily angered or you may learn their ways and find yourself ensnared.*
- *Be wary of those who compliment you unduly for they are your enemy - history has proven it so.*
- *Be wary if you are rich. Friends multiply when wealth abounds and you will not know*

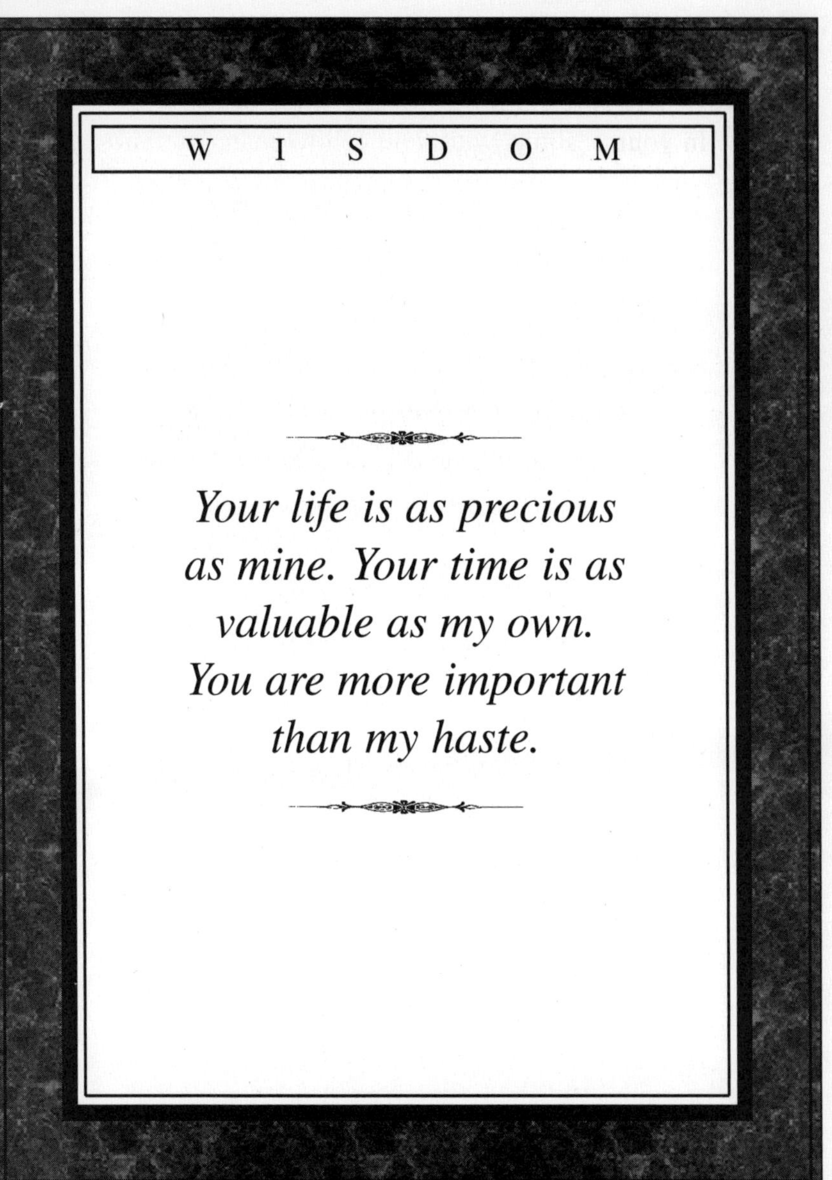
W I S D O M

Your life is as precious as mine. Your time is as valuable as my own. You are more important than my haste.

who your friends are until the tides of fortune change.

- *Do not betray another man's confidence or he who hears it may shame you and you will lose your reputation.*
- *Seldom set foot in your neighbor's house — too much of you and he will grow weary of your voice.*
- *Never put up collateral for your neighbor. It is most likely that foolishness has brought him to this state and it is unlikely that he will listen to wise words or live life in better ways. Help him if you can, but measure generosity with prudence and do not expect to be paid back for the good that you do.*

Solomon's Healing

Illness mirrors the chaos in people's lives.

Years ago, one of the boys I used to know in high school fell asleep at the wheel of his car and ended up in a horrific accident that left him in a coma for nine months. When he finally regained consciousness he was all but a paraplegic.

Due to the constant medical attention he required, he was placed in a local hospice that specialized in treating and rehabilitating patients in his condition as well as caring for and comforting the terminally ill.

Visiting this place always touches me deeply because I know that most patients who arrive through the front door leave through the back door in a hearse.

As I wander the halls I can't help but see what happens at the end for some, and it makes me realize, in *no* uncertain terms, the value of my health. To breathe without struggle or pain, to be able to eat without tubes, to be able to stand and walk — these are truly important and these are what you will miss one day.

I tell you honestly, when you are living these days, you will not miss your car, your spouse, your kids, your money, or anything else for that matter. When your health is gone you won't weep for any of these. You will weep for a lifetime of choices that have left you in this state and you will weep because you will never know solid food again.

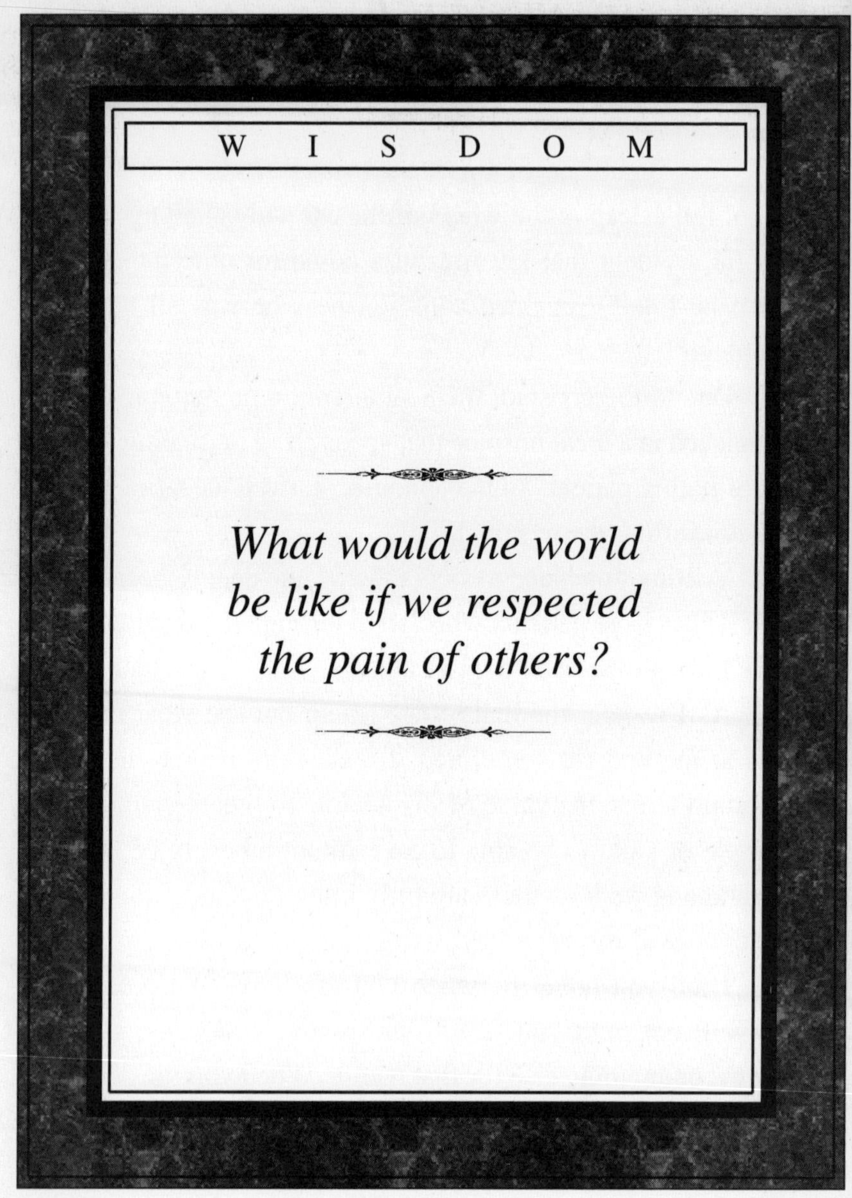
W I S D O M
What would the world be like if we respected the pain of others?

When I leave this place, I feel bed-ridden eyes looking down at me from the windows above and sense their longing as they watch me walk away under my own power.

I leave this place a different person and vow never to take my health for granted again.

* * * *

There was a time when the touch of a hand could heal the sick and the dying.

The only sounds in the dimly lit room would be the raspy shudders of labored breathing and the soft, almost imperceptible steps of a gentle approach.

With perfect humility and timeless serenity, He would sit on the side of the bed as a palpable haze of life and death wafted past His silent prayer.

The beautiful words and emotions that are health would slowly fuse with desires that are born only from empathy, to form a vision of strength and peace that would heal the body and quell the mind.

Then, in mercy, His hand would release faith for one brief moment to rock the cradle of a lost soul and reset the life of an ill existence.

To the people so treated, the incident would slowly fade and leave an indelible vestige of the greatness that had touched them and the knowledge that all that was wrong had been made right again.

Those were good days.

Today, it is different but, in a real sense, we are all

capable of the miracle of healing. There is just more to it now.

Our body manifests our life. Our body listens. On the whole, we create the state of health within us. In illness, more often than not, we are at fault as individuals and if not as individuals, then certainly as a society. We are the sculptors and the clay.

Make every day a work of art.

To maintain or restore health, there is nothing new under the sun. To be healthy, you begin by filling your mind and your environment with strong, uplifting thoughts, emotions and actions. By being the harbinger of a positive life, you redirect the subtle yet powerful voices of the heart and mind. Kind words heal and soothe the soul.

Meditate every day on the fit and healthy person you wish to become. In your visions, feel your body strong and see yourself as a vital and vibrant person. This sows seeds in the silence of the ages where prayer and desire are summoned to fashion the future.

Eat well, exercise, stretch and do everything in moderation and with a thankful heart. This is faith in action and proof of your intent.

As your life begins to change, take a look at the people around you. What they talk about, what they do and what they focus on will influence your life and your health every day. Avoid all evil. Pray. This is wisdom.

It is these simple disciplines that make all the difference. Solomon himself could do no better. Embrace them and your heart will be at peace, your health will return to you and aging will become a soft and subtle crown of glory because life and wisdom will have met in a beautiful crescendo of time and choices.

Shortcuts are illusions.

LIFE, BLESSINGS AND OTHER THINGS

Faith must be tempered with the knowledge that God has plans too.

We would certainly be remiss if we did not briefly wade into that part of life that remains so mysterious.

How long we wait in the deafening silence, straining into the void for the word and for the light. Days turn into weeks, weeks to months. The decades go by and we wait as liars and cheats seem to get ahead in life. Hope long deferred makes the heart sick and the mind ache for a longing fulfilled.

What of the silver spoon, we ask? Everyone strives but few attain. Why do prayers go unanswered? So many of us hope for a better future only to find strife and feel resentment over lost opportunities and misplaced hope. Before long the flame of hope, that burned so brightly when we were children, is extinguished. We give in and we give up. Why them and not us?

Despite being a book of answers, I know not the will of the Father. We are but a grain of sand on a beach, praying that the maker of the beach will heed our calls amidst the endless waves.

What I do know is that those who are truly blessed in this world are merely good stewards of life and as such they lack for nothing. They know that what is quickly attained is seldom blessed in the end, so they strive for slow, measured progress that builds their lives in many ways; and because

W I S D O M

Humility before prayer;
awe before answer.

they are wise with small amounts — the daily amounts — they are given charge over much.

Good stewards know that to build a magnificent life takes time. One brick must be laid upon another with diligence. Shortcuts are illusions.

That which is truly valuable
is not quickly attained.

They know that life is precious; life is short and it is in our nature to overlook value and take it for granted because it is with us daily.

Real blessings are the simple pleasures, and only after they are gone do we see what we had. What we perceive as precious and that which we covet are merely baubles and trinkets that play on our vanity.

* * * *

From the time you were born, you were to be the light of the world. You were born to be the best part of humanity. With every decision you make, you either choose to be the light or choose to be the darkness; there is nothing in between.

To choose the light is to live wisely. The light that wisdom casts will never fail to reveal problems along your path and protect your every step. Where the light is, God is.

Where darkness is, God is not.

Choose a better way. Live by wisdom, live by peace, live by diligence, and live by love. Only then will your prayers be heard and all will be well in your life.

Be patient. Time is impervious to effort.

AN UNHERALDED FUTURE

Tread lightly for you are living on borrowed time and on a borrowed creation.

It troubles me that one can be the salt of the Earth, live the letter of the law, speak gently, tread lightly, live and be the very breath of wisdom itself, and yet still be condemned, slandered, plotted against, and even killed. It has always been this way, it is this way, and it will always be this way.

Knowing this, there may be times when, despite our finest efforts, life is strained beyond the string's capacity, the music stops, and peace becomes a distant memory.

Suffering, during these times, is personal evolution in progress. We are all tested until the bough breaks but where

Even the strongest bend in the fury of a storm; stubborn trees break.

we heal, we become the strongest.

I remember, after a year or so of studying what I have written about in this book, that my life started to change. Though the world remained the same, I began to see through the fog for the first time and life began to make sense. It was then that I knew I had found a small piece of what everyone was looking for. A portion of Eden had survived in wisdom.

W I S D O M
You will be the
salt of the Earth.

The results of free will create time and events that are nothing more than the momentum of consequence exerting itself. Wisdom is consequential genius. Wisdom leaves no trace, only good memories about who you were, about how you did what you did and how you treated others. All other memories speak of a different way.

What can we say about a generation that does not know the appropriate responses to life? We laugh at disasters, we respect and revere the unworthy, and we seem to have an infinite capacity to forget what is truly important. Though looking we do not see; though listening we do not hear or understand.

Wisdom never makes the headlines
because it never destroys the peace.

History repeats itself because our responses to the challenges of life have never changed. As individuals, we all insist on touching the flame to know that fire burns. As a society, we maneuver the ship named history with the same old rudder and history stays the course.

Yet, there is a better way. With wisdom at the helm, we can avoid the predictable storms of life and chart a course to the gentle waters of a better future.

In a wise world, infidelity doesn't happen because respect and understanding averts it, planes don't crash

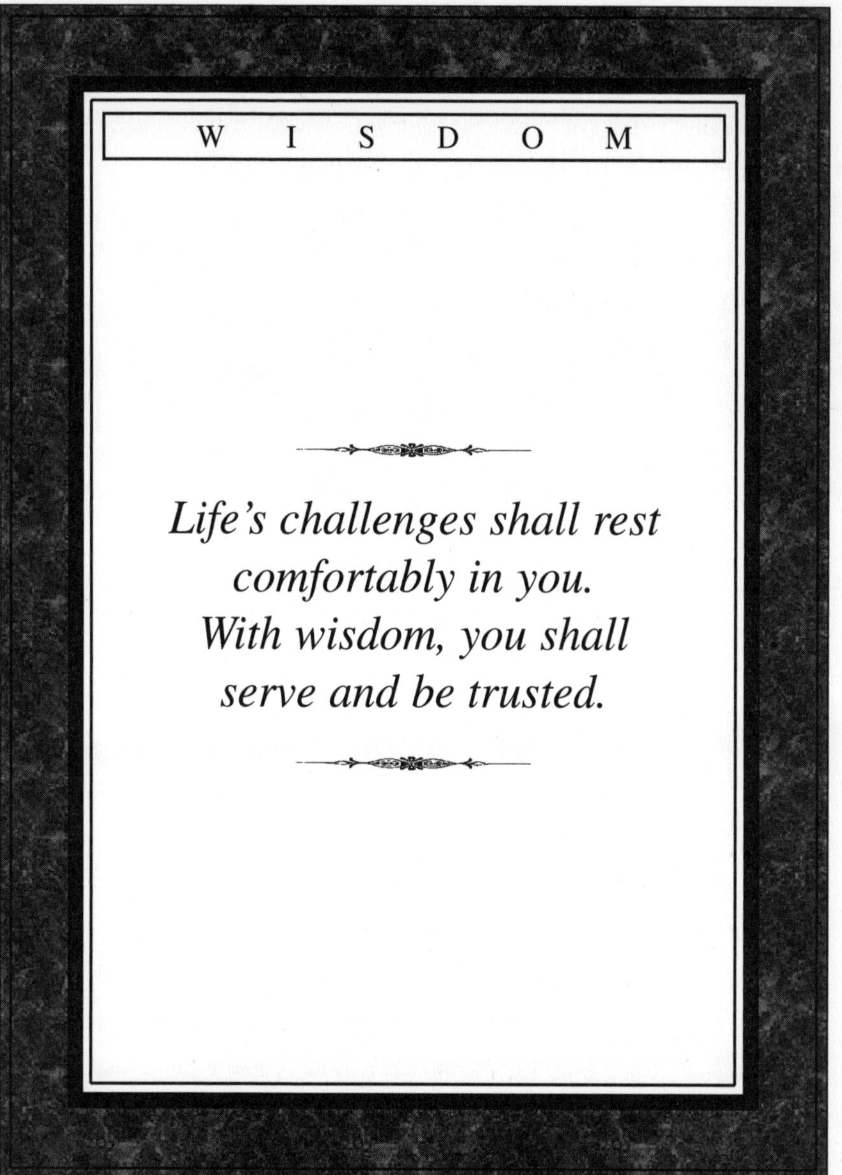

W I S D O M

Life's challenges shall rest comfortably in you. With wisdom, you shall serve and be trusted.

because diligence prevents it, and holocausts don't happen because wisdom never lets evil play the game.

The wise cultivate a magnificent life. All others inherit the façade that is created when vanity plays to ego. Wise people do what others do not, they find what others cannot, and they hear when others have turned a deaf ear.

They clearly see what confuses and dilutes the lives of man and they revel in the mystery and perfection of it all. They pray every day and see the world through ancient eyes.

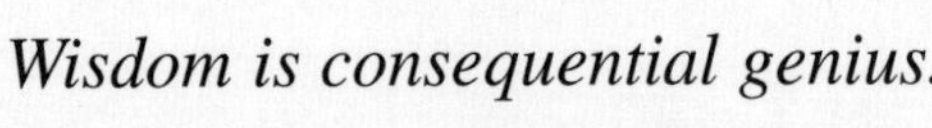

Wisdom is consequential genius.

They will tell you the truth, work diligently, do the job correctly, and always make the right decisions.

They are the salt of the Earth. They are the rocks upon which the world is built. They are the calm in the center of the storm. They are like the fresh air of spring and the cool rain that ends the drought. They refresh the spirit, nurture the soul and bring with them a subtle peace that touches the heart and calms the mind.

Their words are carefully chosen. When they talk to you there is no hidden agenda. There is only honesty. They speak of love and kindness, care and respect. They speak only of what they know and refuse the temptations of gossip. They are quiet, they are silent and because they can be trusted with little, they are inevitably entrusted with much.

WISDOM
In all things, I AM.

They build.

Nothing they do is extraordinary and yet because they do the right thing, what they do is always extraordinary relative to the world around them. They are the masters of life, they are the world's unsung heroes and they are the way it should be.

It is my belief that God has granted us the wisdom found in Proverbs because there is nothing He would rather see than a glorious future, an extraordinary life and more of the way it should be.

Therefore, live your life as if it were art. Take the simple and make it beautiful. Magnify the possibilities. Fulfill all that you are. Be as strong as the mighty oak, bring shade to those who suffer and play in the winds of life. Be wise.

Let the sound of your leaves be as a gentle tongue that brings healing to the weary soul and use your life to help others fulfill themselves. In this way the forests of the future will grow strong.

Know that your roots go back to the beginning of time and all that you are began with the first Word. You truly are of the Father. Live like it.